THE
HOLY GRAIL
OF HOOPS

THE
HOLY GRAIL
OF HOOPS

One Fan's Quest to Buy the Original Rules of Basketball

JOSH SWADE

AFTERWORD BY BILL SELF

SPORTS
PUBLISHING

Sports Publishing books may be purchased in bulk at special discounts for sales promotion, corporate gifts, fund-raising, or educational purposes. Special editions can also be created to specifications. For details, contact the Special Sales Department, Sports Publishing, 307 West 36th Street, 11th Floor, New York, NY 10018 or sportspubbooks@skyhorsepublishing.com.

Sports Publishing® is a registered trademark of Skyhorse Publishing, Inc.®, a Delaware corporation.

Visit our website at www.sportspubbooks.com

10 9 8 7 6 5 4 3 2 1

Library of Congress Cataloging-in-Publication Data
Swade, Josh.
  The holy grail of hoops : one fan's quest the buy the original rules of basketball / Josh Swade.
     pages cm.
  ISBN 978-1-61321-383-4 (hardcover : alk. paper) 1. Basketball--United States--Rules. 2. Basketball--United States--History. 3. Naismith, James, 1861-1939. Basketball. I. Title.
  GV885.55.S93 2013
  796.3230973--dc23
                                    2013013459

Printed in the United States of America

For my mom, who gave me my religion.
And for my dad, who gave me another.

"Though he always had had a great affection for sports, he had been a neutral observer interested more in the game than in loyalty to a single team. But after a time, hardly noticeable at first, he caught something of my enthusiasm for the beauty and permanent character of staying with someone through victory and defeat..."

—Frederick Exley
A Fan's Notes

CONTENTS

AUTHOR'S NOTE

In this book there are many references made to traditional religion. I sincerely hope no one takes offense to these comparisons as they are intended to be more tongue-in-cheek than serious in nature.

But the spiritual side of this story is very real. The truth is there is no way to separate the circumstances surrounding the conception and evolution of the game of basketball from religion. Basketball has proved to be a creation, like the one described in the Bible that has since spawned a new way of life around the world.

Basketball's inventor James Naismith was an extremely religious man. He claimed that the only reason he was offered a position at the University of Kansas was because he knew how to pray. When he arrived at KU, his primary responsibility was to lead the daily chapel service in a 650-seat auditorium. Naismith's religious services were a hit on campus and around town at local Sunday schools, where he frequently led jam-packed prayer groups.

Naismith's disciple Phog Allen was also a very religious man. He too put together a remarkable twenty-five-year career teaching Sunday school. Like Naismith, Allen had enormous enthusiasm for the Bible and even named his first book *My Basket Ball Bible*, which at the time was the most comprehensive book on basketball ever published. Ten years after its release, Phog's *Bible* was out of print, completely sold out, an unheard of distinction for a book catering mainly to coaches and teachers. It had been written. And it had indeed been read.

Allen also brought his sermon into the locker room. Now the pregame pep talk is almost cliché, seen on TV and in countless movies. But back then it was revolutionary. "He'd make you want to run through a brick wall," All-American Clyde Lovellette attested.

"I'd look around the room after one of his speeches and see tears in everyone's eyes," said reserve guard Dean Smith.

With Naismith on his side, Allen would challenge his team. "Only five players get to wear the Kansas jersey," he would say as he looked deep into their eyes. "Are you ready?"

I never met Phog Allen or James Naismith but both of these spiritual men inspired this story and me.

INTRODUCTION: THE JOURNEY

MONDAY, NOVEMBER 1, 2010: 39 DAYS UNTIL AUCTION

That first day of November had felt like every other first day of November I'd ever experienced. I was back from the dead. I felt alive again. It was the dawn of a new college basketball season, and once again there was a reason to get up in the morning, a reason to leave my house, a reason to smile, a reason to feel like anything was possible.

I am a fanatically crazed, insane nut-job for the Kansas Jayhawks, just like my father before me and just like his father before him. The program's prospects for success dominate my thoughts, my time, my happiness, my feelings of self-worth and my overall place in the world. Kansas basketball represents 90 percent of my existence on this planet, with my wife, child, and dog sharing the other 10 percent. Admittedly, I have a huge problem. Let me qualify that. I will admit that it *appears to others*

I have a huge problem. To me, this is not a problem. To me, there is simply no other way to live.

And if there was ever a year to feel optimistic about our chances, this season was it. The Jayhawks were once again the consensus favorite to win the National Championship, and for the second year in a row, were ranked as the preseason number one team in the country. Last year had ended miserably, when in the second round of the NCAA tournament, we suffered a shocking upset to Northern Iowa (a nine seed), ending what was certain to be a run to the title. The loss had sent me into a deep depression. It had made me question my relationships, my religion, and my reason for living.

But time is the great healer. And some offseason recruiting triumphs (Thomas Robinson and Xavier Henry), along with some skilled returning players (Cole Aldrich and Sherron Collins), had me thinking that this was going to be our year. This wasn't just my opinion; it was the opinion of well-respected analysts, renowned writers, noteworthy bloggers, and other fans writing on the message boards I spent most of my life reading. So on the morning of Monday, November 1, 2010, while I should have been hard at work in my office, I decided that I was going to read every last article, paragraph, sentence, and message board post I could find concerning the Jayhawks of Kansas.

Most of what I read that morning had been your typical beginning of the season fare. I read articles on ESPN about the upcoming season, followed by message board posts with links to these same articles, followed by even more message board posts with various fans discussing the merits of these very same articles.

One of the message board posts, however, struck me as unusual. This was a link to the *New York Times* website, a far cry from your typical online sports outlet. It was highly unusual for the *New York Times* to write anything about my beloved Jayhawks. After living in New York for fifteen years, I had all but given up on the local media paying any attention to the greatest basketball program in America. So I clicked on the link, expecting it to be some sort of mistake. But it wasn't. There, on the screen before me, was a familiar picture of basketball's inventor and KU's first coach, Dr. James Naismith. Immediately my curiosity was piqued, as Naismith had been an absolutely seminal figure throughout the course of my entire life.

Sports fans may know that James Naismith invented basketball in 1891 at a YMCA in Springfield, Massachusetts. What most people do not know, however, is that soon after Naismith invented the game, he came to the University of Kansas, where he launched their basketball program. Naismith fell so in love with Lawrence, Kansas, that he spent the final forty-one years of his life there. He is even buried down the road from the university. Growing up in Kansas, I could see his legacy all over town: The Jayhawks play on James Naismith Court, located on a street called Naismith Drive. As a young boy going to KU basketball camp each summer, I lived in a dormitory called Naismith Hall.

As such, I spanned the *New York Times* article with great focus. The headline is one I'll never forget: "Original Rules of Basketball Set to Be Auctioned." What I then proceeded to read struck me as nothing short of impossible: The original rules of basketball, the same ones that hung in the Springfield YMCA gymnasium where James Naismith had invented the game in 1891, were going to be auctioned off at Sotheby's auction house in New York City—just one month later, on December 10.

At first I couldn't wrap my head around what I was reading. I could not comprehend how the original rules of basketball still existed. Here was the birth certificate of a game that had literally changed the world, a sport that had given us Michael Jordan and Magic Johnson, Larry Bird and LeBron James. And now, some 119 years after they were first committed to paper, these rules were set to be auctioned off to the highest bidder.

Thursday, November 4: 36 Days Until Auction

In the four days that had passed since I first read that article, I couldn't get it out of my head. Something about those two old pieces of paper spoke to me. Perhaps I'd seen one too many episodes of *Antiques Roadshow* on PBS, where people were always bringing in what appeared to be worthless artifacts only to find out that they were incredibly valuable. I loved the idea of something so seemingly worthless being essentially priceless.

I tried to imagine what kinds of people would be positioning themselves to win this auction. I had recently watched an HBO documentary, titled *Born Rich,* that depicted one family with generations of wealth who chose to spend their time collecting seminal documents from defining moments in history. They kept these valuable papers in their own private collections for family and friends to casually view from time to time. I wondered if someone like this would win this auction and lock up the rules in a private vault for the rest of eternity, safely away from public consumption.

I then considered how big basketball had become. Perhaps the rules would be secured by someone abroad, perhaps a foreign head of state or maybe an institution like the FIBA Basketball Hall of Fame in Spain. The thought of the rules leaving the United States—its birthplace—was sickening. While basketball was the world's fastest growing sport, it was a game invented on American soil.

If the rules were to stay domestic, I considered some possible stateside destinations. The Basketball Hall of Fame in Springfield, Massachusetts, seemed logical. Or perhaps the Smithsonian in Washington, D.C., would be a fitting depository. After all, it was home to many influential artifacts from American history.

I then thought about the rules from a work standpoint: What would my boss think of this auction? Would she find this story as compelling as I had? I worked as a producer at a TV production company based in New York City. Since most of what we did was sports oriented, it wouldn't be out of the question to run this by her. I wondered if I should send her a link to the *Times* article. She was always encouraging us to bring in ideas, but what exactly was my idea? Could we film the auction, I wondered? Next to the auction, could we tell the story of James Naismith? The story of basketball? The story of America? I decided to email her the link to the article, and wrote that we could do "something glorious on the auction . . . on Naismith . . . on basketball . . . on the American dream." She wrote me back right away.

"Sounds interesting."

I decided to call up Sotheby's and inquire.

Friday, November 5: 35 Days Until Auction

Sotheby's was just down the street from my apartment, and I had never once set foot inside. There was no reason for me to. I couldn't begin to afford anything ever sold at that place. Walking past the mammoth auction house from time to time, I had found the building quite intimidating.

I even felt intimidated to call Sotheby's, like somehow my voice would give away my pathetic bank balance. So when I did call to inquire about the rules, I was pleasantly surprised to be greeted by a friendly voice on the other end. I tried as best I could to explain that I worked at a production company and that I was interested in learning more about the original rules of basketball. Sotheby's PR department informed me of an upcoming "meet the press day," in which the media could meet the seller of the rules and the Sotheby's executive overseeing the auction. They said it would be fine for me to come and meet the Sotheby's curator, but that any arrangements to meet the Naismith family would have to be made on my own, as they could not facilitate such an interview for a non-media outlet.

Figuring it was worth a shot, I decided to try and get in touch with the Naismith family. Searching online, I found a couple of recent articles that had quoted James Naismith's grandson, a man named Ian Naismith, about the upcoming auction. The article stated that Ian was finally selling the rules to bolster the funds of something called the Naismith International Basketball Foundation. The poor economy had decimated the foundation's finances, and left him with no choice but to sell the rules.

I searched online for this Naismith International Basketball Foundation; certain there would be a website through which I could make contact . . . but there wasn't. I could not find a website, headquarters, phone number, address, nor any contact information whatsoever. What I did find was an article from the previous year detailing a visit from this Ian Naismith to a university located in the northeastern United States, where he had ceremoniously displayed the rules for the student body to enjoy. I reached out to the university and was eventually able to wrangle up a cell phone number for Ian Naismith. The woman who gave me the number had no clue if it still worked, and, as I began to dial, I didn't fully expect anyone to answer. When someone finally did, I still thought it was a wrong number. "Hello, I am looking for Mr. Ian Naismith."

"Well," said the voice on the other end, "if you're looking for someone named 'ee-an,' there's no one here by that name. But if you're looking for someone named 'yawn,' you're in the right place."

"Oh . . . I'm sorry," I said. "Are you the one selling the rules of basketball?"

"I sure am," he replied. "What can I do you for?"

I couldn't believe it. I had actually reached a living, breathing Naismith, an heir to the creator of basketball. And here he was on the other end of the phone, wondering who I was.

I paused. I stumbled. I wasn't really sure what to say. I didn't really even know why I was calling.

In some form of broken English, I gave him my name and asked if I could sit down with him at the Sotheby's press day the following week for an interview.

"Well, who you with?" he said.

"Well, I'm not in the press," I told him. "I'm with a TV production company in New York."

I was waiting for the fifth degree. *What do you mean a TV production company? What are you trying to do? Who in the world are you?*

To these questions, I had not one acceptable answer.

But instead, he simply said, "Sounds good. I'll see you in New York."

I hung up, relieved. I could tell I was going to like this Yawn Naismith guy.

1

TRADITION

AS A CHILD, I often felt different because I was Jewish. Growing up in Kansas, hardly anyone was Jewish. In fact, I was the only Jew in my entire grade school.

Now don't get me wrong, my family and I were far from religious. We fell under the Reform classification. Reform Judaism is said to be the most modernized version of Judaism in existence. For us, modernized meant that we hardly ever went to temple.

There were, however, two occasions each year when praying was a must. These, of course, were the Jewish imperatives known as the High Holy Days. The first was Rosh Hashanah, observed in honor of the Jewish New Year. The second was Yom Kippur, known as "The Day of Atonement." On this day, you go to temple to atone for the sins you've committed over the past year.

To describe these rare days of prayer as "enjoyable" would have been a stretch to say the least. But in truth, I didn't mind going to temple, as it meant getting pulled out of school. In Kansas, none of my classmates could understand where I was.

"Were you sick yesterday?" they'd ask.
"No, it was Rosh Hashanah," I would respond.
"Rush-a-what?"
"I was at the synagogue."
"You were where?"

To reach this Reform easy street, where religion conveniently fit into an acceptable two-day-a-year commitment, where all the year's sins could be wiped away with one day of atonement, you must carry out a series of educational prerequisites as an adolescent. These consist of a mixture of Sunday and Hebrew school, the lessons of which grow more intense until they finally culminate in your bar (or bat, for girls) mitzvah, which typically occurs when you are thirteen years of age. Once you go through this ancient ritual, you are showered with money and gifts. Best of all, you have reached the penultimate point in life when you are only required to dedicate two days each year to your religion.

At first, I approached my bar mitzvah like I had approached everything involving Judaism to that point: with tremendous afterthought. This afterthought quickly turned into tremendous anxiety. What at first seemed like something that would never actually happen suddenly became an impending reality. About two months before the big date, in the midst of a mighty Torah struggle, I tried a last-ditch attempt to get out of it once and for all. At the eleventh hour, I tried to convince my dad that this whole bar mitzvah thing had been one big mistake. Below is the gist of my attempt:

Me: Dad, I need to talk to you about my bar mitzvah.
Dad: What about it?
Me: I don't think I can do it.
Dad: Why's that?

*Me: My Torah portion is too difficult. I'm afraid I will fail
   miserably.*
Dad: Just do the best you can, and you'll make us proud.
Me: That's the thing; I'd hate to embarrass the family.
*Dad: I had a bar mitzvah, my dad had a bar
mitzvah . . . you're having a bar mitzvah.*
End of story.

I knew going in that I didn't have a fighting chance. My only hope now was faking a serious injury the night before, knowing even that with the flu, my father would drag me to the pulpit by the back of my new suit, point to the Torah, unraveled before me and say, "read." I considered faking some sort of debilitating sports injury acquired deep in the throes of my daily neighborhood exploits. But even then, at the insistence of my dad, I imagined entering the temple in Willis Reed fashion, miraculously pulling off a stirring rendition of my Torah portion, followed by the first standing ovation ever given in the history of Temple B'nai Jehudah.

There was simply no way I was getting out of it. His father had done it, he had done it, and so my inevitable journey down the same path was sealed. I was up against centuries of tradition. And to my father, nothing was more important than tradition. "Tradition this, tradition that," everything with him was "tradition." Channeling some version of the Broadway star Zero Mostel, he would often sing the song "Tradition" from *Fiddler on the Roof*, as if it was the defining soundtrack to his life. "How do we keep balance in life?" he would belt. "Tradition, tradition . . . tradition!"

A week before my bar mitzvah, feeling the most Jewish I ever had in my life, I decided to press my dad for answers. "What is Judaism? Where does it come from? How did this tradition get started?"

He thought for a minute. He paused. He thought some more. He finally said, "Go study your Torah portion."

It was clear he didn't know.

I then went down to our TV room and found the VHS tape of *Fiddler on the Roof.* I put it in the VCR, hopeful for some answers. The main character named Tevye was the father of five, just like my dad. I watched as Tevye broke into the infamous "Tradition" song.

"How do we keep our balance?" said Tevye. "That I can tell you in one word . . . 'tradition.'"

"We have traditions for everything," Tevye continued. "How to sleep. How to eat. How to work. How to wear clothes. For instance we always keep our heads covered; this shows our constant devotion to God."

"You may ask," Tevye continued. "How did this tradition get started?"

Yes, I thought. How did this tradition get started?

"I'll tell you," said Tevye, a serious expression coming over his face.

Tevye paused. He thought again.

"I don't know," said Tevye.

I couldn't believe it. Even the guy from *Fiddler* didn't know.

"But it's a tradition," he continued. "And because of our tradition, everyone knows who he is and what God expects him to do."

2

THE OTHER RELIGION

THE LAWS OF Judaism are very clear and straightforward. They simply state that if your mother is Jewish, then you are Jewish. Your father's religious background matters none. And since my mother was Jewish, it was her and her alone I had to thank for being Jewish.

But from my father, I received another religion altogether. Unlike Judaism, this was a faith we took a very active role in, especially from November to March. For this religion, we were all too eager to go to temple, close our eyes, clench our fists, and vigorously pray. It was a religion that brought tremendous highs into our lives. But it was also a belief system that brought the lowest of lows, in shocking fashion, almost yearly. In the end, we felt our commitment to Kansas basketball, in all of its bipolar glory, was worth it.

Before my bar mitzvah, I had pressed my dad on the origins of Judaism, which had found him at a loss for words. As a child, I also went to my father and asked him about the origins of Kansas basketball. To this he responded with a diatribe, a thesis, a history lesson of epic proportions. Were it not for things like sleep or work or eating, he likely never would have stopped talking.

My father's feelings for Kansas basketball had always been tremendously strong, his passion downright contagious. He made it very clear: Jayhawk basketball was as life and death as sports could get. Things such as happiness, self-worth, and your place in the world all depended on the outcome of these games. My brother Micah and I couldn't help but to be sucked in . . . and once we caught the bug, we were a small army of KU fanatics adept in every detailed nuance of cheering for the Jayhawks. Decked out head-to-toe in crimson and blue attire, we quickly became experts in the various fan rituals. We "waved the wheat" (swayed back and forth like wheat blowing in the wind), sang the alma mater ("Far above the golden valley . . ."), and chanted the famous Rock Chalk Chant ("Rock, Chalk, Jayhawk, KU"). Even my mother was pleased to see we were spending quality time with our father, albeit in a frenzied, uncontrolled state of emotion.

The annual "Late Night" event, the first practice of the year opened to the public, became our true New Year's celebration, our real Rosh Hashanah. From November to December, we were devoted followers astute in our daily prayer. Once conference play began in January, we were dedicated followers; you could even say religious zealots. And once the season culminated with conference tournaments and the high stakes NCAA Tournament, we were akin to religious extremists.

Each Monday night, we sat around the dinner table and listened intently to "Hawk Talk," the local radio call-in show with the head coach. Most nights at the dinner table were filled with uncontrollable noise and commotion: five young kids fighting to be heard. But on Monday night, no one spoke about his or her day at school, dance class, baseball team, or life even. On this night, no one dared to say a word. We would all sit quietly and listen to the coach, with my dad, Micah, and I hanging on his every word.

Dad taught us about the game of basketball and the strategy behind different offensive and defensive schemes. Phrases like "man-to-man," "fast break," "zone," and "full court press" became part of our regular vocabulary. He taught us about the current players and highlighted their strengths and weaknesses. We screamed with ecstasy when they succeeded and yelled with frustration when they failed. My dad didn't know how to hold back his emotions, so neither did we. All preconceived socially acceptable roles between parents and children were thrown out the window for these two hours. It would not have been uncommon for my brother and me to curse out the officials. "That was a bullshit call," he would say. "Fucking refs," I would reply.

In between games, at bedtime, in the car, anywhere we found ourselves with some spare time, Dad taught us about the history of Kansas basketball. He'd recall the greats before his time. He'd tell us stories about the legends from his youth. Whenever he'd speak of this tradition, it would be with a careful intensity. It was clear to us that this was not something to be taken lightly. This was "something to be cherished," he told us, a reason to be proud of who we were and where we came from.

Had my old man displayed the same passion for Judaism that he displayed for Kansas basketball, I'm quite certain that today I would be a rabbi or cantor, leading a congregation or perhaps living in Israel leading a life dedicated to God. But he didn't.

Our holy land was located in Lawrence, Kansas—not Jerusalem, and our temple, our shrine, our place of worship, was the unrivaled, incomparable, unmatched college basketball arena known as Allen Fieldhouse.

Allen Fieldhouse had been KU's home arena since 1955, and was a huge part of what made Kansas basketball so unique. If religious ceremonies and spiritual gatherings are meant to take place in awe-inspiring structures, Allen accomplished this to absolute perfection. This was a place of ageless splendor, its walls confining its timeless beauty. This was basketball's Pantheon, its Duomo, its St. Patrick's Cathedral all rolled into one.

In fact, the confines of Allen Fieldhouse were so coveted, so sought after, that it was literally impossible to get inside. Every ticket for every game was not only spoken for, but the waiting list for season tickets was a mile long. For years my dad tried, best he could, to secure tickets using every possible angle he could think of. But each time the result would be the same . . . nothing.

Then our luck changed. When I turned ten years old, my dad finally pulled off the impossible. Through a business associate, he was able to get tickets for two bench seats high up in the corner. But their location didn't matter; we had found a way in. From that point on, I spent every home game next to my dad, packed like a sardine in a can, and loving every minute of it.

My newfound status as a season ticket holder was evident even within the halls of my grade school. Actually, having tickets to the games separated me from the pack; all of a sudden, I was placed on a pedestal. At the lunch table, my classmates would invariably discuss the players, the coaching staff, and forecast the season. Without fail, disagreements would ensue. But when I, the season ticket holder, spoke up, everyone paid close attention. After all, I got to go inside of Willy Wonka's chocolate factory . . . again and again and again.

Because what these tickets represented was so monumental, we treated their arrival with the utmost of importance. Each September, we'd eagerly wait for their arrival. The university always managed to up the ante each season with artistic takes on real scenes from Kansas basketball lore. Covered with painted faces of past KU greats, each ticket was a miniature LeRoy Neiman in itself.

Today, team schedules surface way in advance, often posted on the Internet a year before the season begins. But back then, we didn't know the schedule until the tickets arrived. Once they would arrive, we would scan them, looking for upcoming games of importance, imagining what would be at stake at that point in the season. There was invariably the Missouri matchup, a rivalry game that we heavily anticipated each year—one that always brought out the most venom from the collective KU nation. There was also the in-state rivalry game with Kansas State, who'd become a laughing stock among KU faithful. This had become a rivalry that was so one-sided, it was barely a rivalry, but more a reminder of just how good it was to be a Jayhawk and how bad it could be to support the Wildcats (or anyone else for that matter). There were also the non-conference games against the other big name schools. It seemed like each year there was one of these games against an Indiana, UCLA, or Kentucky. These were the games we coveted, highlighted on the calendar, and built our winter schedules around. If family vacations were ever discussed, we first referred to the schedule. If play dates were suggested, we compared them to the schedule. If wedding, birthday, or holiday party invitations were extended, we checked the schedule.

The forty-five-minute drive from Kansas City to Lawrence always seemed to take twice as long on game days. Whether we were playing Indiana or the Indianapolis School for the Blind, I could not wait to get inside the Fieldhouse to take it all in. There was very little dialogue between Dad and me on those trips. We both spent the time listening closely to the radio's pregame show as it blared through the car speakers. After parking, we'd sit in the lot and listen to the head coach's interview. Once it was complete, we'd race into the Fieldhouse, arriving at our seats, high in the corner, just before tip-off.

Game after game, year after year, one thing never changed: the excitement of going to games in Allen Fieldhouse. Even after being inside this fantastic basketball museum many times, your memory—vivid as it may be—did the place no justice. Only in a relaxed state of sleep could your dreams capture the smells, the students, the sights, and the sounds. It was the greatest show on earth (in Kansas at least), and every time you walked in, it felt like you were home . . . and you were.

As great as it was to share this experience with my dad, I couldn't wait until I was old enough to attend KU and be a part of the student section. To me, the student section was a thing of beauty. I had watched them closely my entire youth, first on TV and then up close. During games I would find myself watching the students instead of watching the action on the court. I was their biggest fan. All the traditions: the singing of the alma mater, the rock chalk chant, free throw disruptions on opposing teams, I loved them all. I knew that one day I would be with them, looking up at my dad in the corner after every big play. With my younger brother Micah getting older, I knew someday soon he would have to take my place alongside my dad.

I had the entire thing planned out at the tender age of fourteen. I would live in Naismith Hall, which was located right across the street from Allen Fieldhouse, on a street known as Naismith Drive. Living in Naismith Hall and crossing Naismith Drive to enter Allen Fieldhouse would be like living in basketball heaven . . . and I couldn't wait for that day to come.

The Journey

Thursday, November 11: 29 Days Until Auction

I grabbed an eager intern from my office and headed uptown to Sotheby's to meet my friend Daymion. Daymion was my best friend living in New York. We had met several years prior when, by complete chance, he answered a newspaper ad for a vacant room my buddies and I had available in our Queens row house. Daymion moved in and had remained my roommate for over five years. Over the course of that period, I had turned the England-born, Boston-bred, UMass grad into an enormous Kansas basketball fan. I wanted Daymion to join me at Sotheby's because I knew he'd enjoy meeting the offspring of James Naismith. But in reality, he was the only person I knew who would film the interview for free. I was taking a risk using Daymion, who worked as an accomplished still photographer and not a video cameraman. He was far from a film expert, but with no budget to speak of, he was the best option I had. "Just hit 'record,'" I told him as we entered the glass monstrosity that is Sotheby's.

After checking in at the front desk, we were told to take a seat and wait. We waited and waited and waited some more, while those with proper media credentials were whisked up to the executive offices for the Naismith Press Day. After a couple hours of waiting, assuming that they had forgotten we were there, a young man in his twenties finally came to greet us. We were led to a back elevator bank and escorted to an empty room high in the sky, where we waited some more.

Eventually, an older, heavy-set man walked in wearing a collared shirt embroidered with a Naismith International Basketball Foundation logo. The minute he opened his mouth to say hello, I recognized him as Ian Naismith, the man I'd spoken to the week before. After shaking Ian's hand, I nervously jumped right into the interview, unversed in the smooth transitions known to a seasoned reporter. I pulled out a set of questions I had carefully prepared the night before and tried my best to put forth an air of professionalism. I wanted to learn about the history of these rules and why after all these years, they would be leaving the hands of the Naismith family.

As I would learn that day, Ian was the youngest son of James Sherman (Jimmy) Naismith, who was the youngest son of James Naismith, which made Ian the youngest living grandchild of basketball's creator. Ian was born in 1938, just a year before his grandfather passed away.

After creating the rules in 1891, Naismith took the two pages with him to the Denver YMCA where he worked for three years while attending medical school. The pages first sat in his desk at the Denver YMCA and then in his desk drawer in Robinson Gymnasium on the campus of the University of Kansas. In the mid 1920s, the rules had no value—except to James Naismith of course—who mounted them on cardboard in preparation to frame and hang them on his office wall. For some reason, Naismith never got around to it, and tucked the rules away back into his desk, safely away from potential years of harmful sunlight. (The cardboard would prove to play an important part in keeping the pages intact and sides from fraying.)

Finally, in the 1930s, with the sport deeply ingrained in the fabric of America, Naismith heard from the Smithsonian that they were interested in acquiring the seminal document. Naismith thought about it but was not so quick to oblige, thinking instead there might be a more suitable place for the rules to end up. More so than James Naismith, his two sons, the older Jack and the younger Jimmy, could foresee the rules' future importance. Jimmy had a hunch that one day the rules would be even more coveted. So in June of 1931, he asked his father to sign the rules to properly authenticate them. James obliged and wrote on the rules with his signature and the date. The following year, James and his eldest son, Jack, took a road trip back east and with them took the rules. They first went by the Springfield College, which had grown from the YMCA Training School where Naismith had invented the game over forty years before. The basketball coach there, Edward Hickox, said he didn't want the rules. They then drove to McGill University in Canada, where Naismith had received both his bachelor's and seminary degrees. But McGill didn't want the rules either. "I guess they are not good for anything," Naismith chuckled, and the two returned to Lawrence with the rules in hand.

In 1937, Naismith half retired from his professor post at KU and his emeritus status brought on a plethora of newfound free time. Ill fitted to just sit back in a rocking chair at his Lawrence home, Naismith took to the preacher circuit, visiting the small rural towns of Kansas and giving stirring sermons on the merits of clean and honest living. Ian's father, Jimmy, was twelve years younger than the next child, and because of this, much of the legwork fell to him. He drove his father from town to town while the elder preacher went from church to church spreading his gospel. This was a period of great bonding between Naismith and his youngest child, and the two became very close.

When Naismith passed away in 1939, his youngest son naturally inherited the rules. Jimmy soon married and moved his wife and three kids to Corpus Christi, Texas. One of those kids was Ian, and by the time he was five years old, the rules sat in the secret drawer of a wooden desk that his handy grandfather had constructed years prior. Ian and his siblings were very obedient and never told anyone of the special paper hiding in the secret drawer out back.

With money tough to come by during the depression of the '30s, Jimmy and his wife transported their kids back and forth through the plains. From their ranch in Corpus Christi to a farmstead in Holton, Kansas, to a house in Gilman, Colorado, to another ranch in Westcliffe, Colorado—wherever the Naismith family went, so too did the rules. In the 1950s, after the war had ended, the Naismiths arrived back in Corpus Christi, where Jimmy decided to finally lock the rules up in a safety deposit box at the local bank.

In 1961, 100 years after James Naismith's birth, the Naismith Memorial Basketball Hall of Fame was under construction in Springfield, Massachusetts. Jimmy went to Springfield to see if they might have any desire for the rules. It turns out that one of the executives of this new landmark was none other than Edward Hickox, the former Springfield coach who'd showed no interest in the rules some thirty years prior. This time, however, Hickox wanted them and so too did Lee Williams, the Hall of Fame's director. Jimmy wrote to the Hall of Fame executives that he would be "discussing the disposition of the rules with my children and will let you know when we have reached an agreement." Ian and his siblings concurred with their father that the Hall of Fame should indeed have the rules to proudly display for all to see. Hickox and Jimmy struck a deal, signing a one-page loan-agreement that explicitly stated that the rules "are the property of the Party of the First Part (James Sherman Naismith) and shall so remain."

In 1995, twenty-seven years after the Hall of Fame was given the rules, Ian went on a crusade to get them back. Ian's reasons for doing so were simple: In twenty-seven years, the Hall of Fame had never once displayed them. While a framed replica had indeed hung in the main lobby, the original version had been safely kept in a vault inside the director's office. As it turns out, the Hall felt that displaying the rules presented too much of a security risk. "The buildings weren't the most secure and a display would have been prohibitively expensive," said Joe O'Brien, who succeeded Williams as executive director of the Hall.

"The Hall told us that if we wanted to donate a display case, it would cost $7,300," Ian said after he retrieved the rules. "I don't think so," he added. Since they were clearly the property of the Naismith family, on September 8, 1995, Ian retook possession of the rules.

For the next fifteen years, Ian and his wife Renee used the rules as the cornerstone of their Naismith International Basketball Foundation. Ian had traveled the country for years, which he marketed as the "Naismith Sportsmanship Tour," where he would exhibit the rules at university functions, Final Fours, and NBA All-Star weekends—all in an effort to halt what Ian referred to as "the deterioration of the game."

In addition to the Sportsmanship Tour, Ian and Renee would make regular trips to the Caribbean, where they'd visit orphanages, bringing clothes and basketballs to groups of needy children. In 2007, Renee, who had long been the heart and soul of the foundation, passed away after a long bout with cancer. With the economy in a recession, the foundation had lost the bulk of its financial support. Waning resources meant Ian could no longer fund the orphaned children like he had in the past. So he concluded that it was time to sell the rules and replenish the funds of his fragile foundation. Ian had hand-selected Sotheby's based on their expert staff in the field of historic documents and their nearly 300-year reputation as the largest, most powerful auction house in the world.

Interviewing Ian Naismith had answered many of my questions. I now understood where the rules had been for 119 years and why they were finally coming up for auction. I had a hunch that this auction was a big deal, and with the Sotheby's sales estimate at over $2 million, it was clear that they felt the same way.

But now I had more questions. Why exactly were two pieces of paper, even ones this old, expected to fetch so much money? What sorts of people did they expect to bid on the rules? And finally and most importantly, where was their most likely resting home? For these questions I would have to hear from Sotheby's themselves. So after Ian and I exchanged our goodbyes, Selby Kiffer, Sotheby's Senior Vice President of Historic Books and Manuscripts, was the next in line to humor me.

I recognized Selby from *Antiques Roadshow* on PBS. He had joined Sotheby's in 1985, and in his twenty-five years, he had worked his way up to become a leader in the field of historic American documents. During his tenure, he had brought hundreds of millions of dollars worth of American treasures to auction. If anyone had seen pieces of paper sell for inconceivable amounts, it was this guy. "It's just words on paper," I said. "Why is it so valuable?"

"Well, everything that's important in modern history comes down to words on paper," said Kiffer. "Whether it's the Magna Carta or the Declaration of Independence. This is the birth of one of the most popular games in the world. Without these two pages, hundreds of millions of people wouldn't have enjoyed playing or watching basketball the way they have over the last twelve decades."

As he continued to answer questions, my stereotypical vision of Selby Kiffer began to unfold. I imagined a man who spent most evenings sipping a perfectly aged red wine in the study of his Upper West Side townhouse with classical music playing wistfully in the background. The way in which he continued to explain the rules' profound importance had an almost poetic cadence to it. Without any trace of ego or phoniness, Kiffer gave off an air of complete and utter wisdom. He wasn't there to sell; he was there to state the facts. A man armed with endless amounts of information and data, which with the greatest of ease he could form into the most eloquent explanations, even for the layman to decipher. If Ian Naismith was a self-described "hillbilly," who'd spent most of his life traveling the back roads of the Great Plains, Selby Kiffer was the exact opposite. One couldn't imagine any circumstance where these two men would come together, other than at the intersection of commerce such as this.

Interviewing Ian had raised my excitement level because of his legendary heritage and my enormous love for basketball. But the more I spoke to Kiffer, the more excited I became about the rules and what they represented. "As an American cultural achievement, it's as innovative as jazz, as pervasive as Hollywood. Wherever you go around the globe you can find basketball," Kiffer said.

It was clear that Selby Kiffer did not see the rules as sports memorabilia. "I almost hate to think of Naismith's rules of basketball as a sports document, because that almost sounds too limiting." And his peers at Sotheby's agreed. The rules would be sharing the stage with the Emancipation Proclamation signed by Abraham Lincoln and a battle flag from General Custer's last stand. On December 10, 2010, three American treasures would be sold at auction.

But still I wondered, "as far as sports go, is this the most important document in world history?"

"In terms of simply being a sports document, yes, nothing else like this exists that captures the origin, the birth of a sport. There have been great contracts sold. We've sold some great letters by famous ballplayers like Ty Cobb and Babe Ruth. But for something that crystallizes a moment of such overwhelming magnitude, I think this stands alone."

As Selby and I wrapped up, the same young man who had escorted us upstairs walked in again. At first, I figured it was a sign that my little dream run was over, that the jig was up. But I was wrong . . . it had only just begun. In his hands, this young man was holding what I immediately made out to be the original rules of basketball: two pieces of almost gold paper surrounded on all sides by white cardboard. My eyes lit up as he walked them over and handed them to me. As I held them, the words jumped off the page. "Basket Ball," written in ink at the top of the page, with thirteen typed rules that spanned two pages. At the bottom of the second page was the infamous line handwritten by Naismith, "First draft of basketball rules hung in the gym so the boys might learn the rules."

But the 119-year-old patina seemed to say so much more than the typed words ever could. The pages screamed of significance. Even to the naked eye it was clear: These were scrolls of biblical proportions. These were not simply the do's and don'ts of a new game. This was the story of a game and a nation—in all of its beautiful evolution.

I thought back to what Selby Kiffer had said to me just a few moments prior. "I hope they end up with someone who appreciates them. I love private collectors. I'm not saying I wouldn't be thrilled to see it go to a great institution. The Smithsonian, obviously the Naismith Hall of Fame, would all be great depositories. Or," he continued, "a great university with a strong basketball tradition." As we wrapped up and said our goodbyes, Selby's last sentence played over and over in my head.

Daymion and I walked quietly and quickly out of Sotheby's, neither one of us wanting to give away our amateur excitement. It felt like we had just pulled off an impossible heist. The interview footage in our hands felt like the nuclear codes. Once safely around the corner we ballyhooed like school girls:

Me: "That was amazing!"

> *Daymion: "Dude!"*
> *Me: "I held the rules!"*
> *Daymion: "Dude!"*
> *Me: "I held the rules!"*
> *Daymion: "Dude!"*

I raced back to the office and watched the footage. I opened up my computer and began typing up a pitch. Paying tribute to the religion spawned from the thirteen rules, I brilliantly called it "The Thirteen Commandments." I proposed that we could produce a piece that would tell the story of basketball, while we built towards this monumental auction, climaxing with the bidding on December 10th. I shot off the proposal to my boss, who was in Los Angeles on business. Still, I expected her to reply immediately with the same excitement that I was certain had jumped off the pages of my pitch. I waited and waited and waited . . . and didn't hear back.

As the next couple of days passed, I considered the idea I had written up. With some healthy separation from the Sotheby's high, something was now crystal clear: My proposal sucked. It was boring. The history of basketball, blah, blah, blah. I wasn't Ken Burns. We didn't create four-day docu-series to air on PBS. Chances were that even I, a self-proclaimed basketball junkie, wouldn't sit through the snooze-fest I had proposed. I waited for my boss to return to New York and in the meantime tried to think of a better idea.

Friday, November 12: 28 Days Until Auction

The voice in my head kept growing louder. In my life, I have never been able to ignore the voice in my head. It had quite often led me down challenging paths. Almost always, the easiest option was to ignore it. But once again, I just couldn't do it.

This voice said, in no uncertain terms, that James Naismith's original rules of basketball, the same ones that hung in the YMCA Gymnasium in Springfield, Massachusetts, on December 21, 1891, the day he invented the game, did not belong back in Springfield at the Basketball Hall of Fame. This voice said the rules, the same ones that represented America's great contribution to world sport, did not belong at the Smithsonian in Washington, DC. This voice said the rules, the greatest sports document in the history of the world, did not belong in the personal archives of some wealthy document collector. This voice said the rules, the same ones that sat in James Naismith's Robinson Gymnasium desk for almost forty years, belonged in one place, and one place only: the University of Kansas.

But was this auction even on the radar of the Jayhawk Nation? Where was the school in all of this? At the very least, I decided that I had no choice but to call the university and see if they even knew that the rules would finally be leaving the Naismith family. If I couldn't get anyone on the phone (which I figured would be the case), at least I would have tried—and perhaps that attempt would be enough to satiate the voice in my head.

Much to my surprise, I was able to reach an associate athletic director. I immediately asked him about the auction. He said that the athletic department did in fact know about the upcoming auction, but there had been no discussion to put together any sort of plan . . . nor would there be. Our conversation was finished almost as soon as it started.

I wondered for a moment if perhaps this university official was not being entirely truthful. If the university was putting together a plan to win the rules, they sure as hell weren't going to tell some random fan living in New York. But the more I thought about it, and the more I considered the certainty in his voice, the more I believed him. Being no stranger to the never-ending laundry list of initiatives that exist inside the athletic departments of public universities, I imagined procuring two pieces of paper for millions of dollars was not exactly identified as a top priority. Certainly an athletic department—even the odd one with a cash surplus—could not possibly spend departmental funds at auction. And even if such a purchase would be approved by first the chancellor and second the Board of Regents, the questionable ethics of using state funds for such a purchase would surely cause tremendous backlash among the non-sports crowd more concerned with funding the university's primary objective: education.

Athletic departments at major universities have a lot on their minds: student athletes, non-revenue sports, facility improvements, retaining coaching talent, and relieving underperforming coaches to name a few. In the big business that is college athletics there is plenty to consider—and it just so happened at that moment, KU had even more to worry about.

Over a year prior, an elaborate scam was uncovered involving several members of the athletic department, and more specifically, those in the basketball ticketing office. A handful of employees had been found guilty of scalping much-coveted Kansas basketball tickets by funneling them to aftermarket ticket brokers and pocketing the proceeds. The scam cost the university millions in lost revenue and had severely damaged their reputation in the eyes of the alumni and donors they counted on. The athletic director at the time was a man named Lew Perkins, who ironically had often been praised for his leadership—namely his fundraising efforts—since arriving at Kansas in 2004. When reports of wrongdoing first surfaced, Perkins denied any knowledge or involvement. Perkins also was not implicated in the subsequent FBI investigation. Ultimately, however, the scandal happened on his watch and proved too much for him to overcome. Perkins finally resigned and a shattered athletic department tried to pick up the pieces and move on.

KU immediately made assurances that they would not rush into hiring a new AD. This time, they would make sure to get the right guy, a guy whose ethical fortitude could restore the department's trust within the community. Perkins had come from the East Coast and was viewed by many as a high roller, a larger than life figure who operated his department in an extravagant manner. After his departure, the school named an interim departmental head and began a methodical search for a new director with less baggage.

It had been five months since Perkins's resignation, and with KU on the verge of another great year in basketball, the sports media had finally begun to paint KU in a positive light. But the day before I called the school to inquire about the auction, federal indictments had come down, formally charging five former KU officials, alleging they pulled in between $3 and $5 million in illegal proceeds. All five individuals were looking at thirty years in federal prison. The grand jury indictments once again brought the ticket scandal front and center, and every major media outlet—including ESPN—ran headlines with the news. With the auction a few weeks away, I had found the KU athletic department at the worst time of their 100-year history.

At first it seemed that a shell-shocked athletic office without an athletic director and a sheer lack of interest in the rules would all but finally put the voice in my head to rest. And it did . . . for a couple hours. But the voice finally spoke up again and said four words: "You don't need them."

Saturday, November 13: 27 Days Until Auction

The weekend had come and I still hadn't heard from my boss, but I knew she was back in town. The voice now owned me. I had tried to get into my usual weekend routine: sleep late, watch basketball, play basketball, and spend hours online reading about basketball . . . but the voice wouldn't let me. The voice said I had to do something. I had to find some way to get these rules home to Lawrence. This opportunity would never present itself again. Once they were sold to someone like the Smithsonian, it would be over forever. So I spent my entire Saturday putting together a plan.

How could I possibly raise enough money in three weeks to have a shot at winning this thing? The answer was obvious: Locate KU alums that, like me, have a titanic passion for Kansas basketball. But I needed alums that had something I didn't have: money. Even if I could find these people and somehow get in front of them, I couldn't just leave to go see them. I had responsibilities: a wife, a child, a mortgage. I also had a job, and it was a critical time at my company, as we were on the verge of beginning to shoot an independent film.

But I needed to leave my home. I needed to leave my job. I needed to at least try. I called my boss, Maura, and told her that

I had to come see her this weekend, and that it was an emergency. The urgency in my voice likely suggested that this couldn't possibly be work related. Maura had hired me over a year ago and taken a chance on bringing me on. I had come to New York to work in the music business, and since graduating college, had pieced together a career moving from record companies to talent agencies to eventually realizing my dream of launching my own record label. The label had been a labor of love, a constant uphill battle . . . moments of incredible momentum, often coupled with periods of incredible frustration. After nearly five years of fighting and clawing, faced with an entire industry in flux, it had become increasingly difficult to make a living. I had been ready for a new challenge. I wanted to stay in the entertainment business, but try my hand at something else. Years prior, I had worked in the music department of the famed William Morris Agency. William Morris, a tradition-rich firm synonymous with the entertainment industry for over 100 years, had proved to be a grad school of sorts. There, I was exposed to many facets of the entertainment business, so when I arrived at Maura's TV production house, Maggie Vision, I felt relatively prepared. I knew she saw something in me, perhaps a bit of herself. Maura had spent over twenty years in the sports television business, having emerged as one of the most successful female producers in the industry. She had done it with hard work. She had done it with passion. I knew that if anyone would respond to passion, it would be Maura.

Sunday, November 14: 26 Days Until Auction

I knew that Sunday was the day. I had called Daymion the day before to tell him that I needed his company on this trip. He too had seen the rules, and could vouch for the awesomeness that emanated from them.

I jumped in Daymion's car and we headed downtown to Maura's apartment. Two blocks down 2nd Avenue, I remembered that I had forgotten something. Daymion, still unsure as to why he was there in the first place, turned around as I ran back into my apartment and grabbed my yarmulke. This was the same one I wore at my bar mitzvah over twenty years prior, and I had hardly worn it since but held onto it because it was given to me as a gift from my parents for that special day. It had been inscribed with my biblical name, "Joshua." On top, my mom had sewn a symbol of my faith. Not the Star of David that so commonly adorned Jewish-themed clothing, but stitched to the top of my yarmulke was a little Jayhawk. As I nervously made my way to the front of the congregation in 1988, scared that I would absolutely blow it, my genius parents knew a Jayhawk would see me through.

I killed my bar mitzvah. Not one mistake. And now I knew it was time to kill this. This too was religious. These were the holy basketball commandments, and I, Joshua, was being called on to bring them home. Because of my tradition, I knew what was expected of me. For Maura to truly understand how this touched my soul, my entire being, my trusty yarmulke was a necessary prop.

I burst into Maura's apartment like a coach would a locker room before a big game. I channeled the great ones: Vince Lombardi, Knute Rockne, Bear Bryant. I explained that the rules were the rightful property of the Jayhawk Nation. I explained that I was being called on like Moses before me to deliver the commandments of basketball back to Mount Oread (the hill which the

University of Kansas sits upon). I explained that I would need a month off of work to try and make this dream a reality.

Maura thought for a moment and said, "You can't have a month off from work."

I felt an uncomfortable choice coming. How was I going to explain to my wife that I had quit my job to go find someone to help me win an auction for two pieces of paper that were 119 years old?

"You can't have time off, but you can go try to make this happen."

"I can?"

"Take a camera along, this could be a great story," she said.

"Who's going to film it?" I asked.

"Daymion," she said looking in his direction.

"I am?"

Monday, November 15: 25 Days Until Auction

I decided to spend one week in the office working the phones. My hope was that this would be sufficient time for me to line up enough meetings so Daymion and I could hit the road. I knew those meetings had to be with people of influence and wealth. On Monday morning, I rolled into work bright and early. "Who's got money and loves Kansas basketball?"

I began calling up my old network of friends and family in Kansas who might be able to put me on to such people. Most everyone I called said I was crazier than they thought, that now I had really lost my mind. Their doubt fueled me on. "You haven't seen crazy," I thought.

"Who supports KU athletics?" My path felt incredibly complex, so much so that I had no idea where to start, how to start, or what to do. My immediate network had given me no leads at all.

I thought of the Jayhawk Nation. If everyone knew what I was trying to do, they'd surely donate to the cause. The hundreds of thousands of fans that span the country would surely pitch in $20, $30, or $40 each to bring the rules home. I decided that I needed a website to get the word out. I called a friend who built websites and put him on the task. We settled on bringtheruleshome.com.

When thinking of a logical resting place for the rules, I immediately thought of the KU campus and Allen Fieldhouse. I thought of the recent renovations and the beautiful new Hall of Fame connected to the stoic hoops cathedral. I imagined the rules sitting in that Hall of Fame; the finishing touch; the cherry on top of the recent facelift that had so perfectly modernized the Fieldhouse while allowing it to maintain all of its history and charm.

I then remembered that the new Hall had some sort of name attached to it. I jumped on Google and searched. "The Booth Family Hall of Athletics." *Who's the Booth Family?*, I wondered. Through more research, I learned that in 2005, the Booth Family had donated millions to construct the Hall of Athletics, which exhibited and honored the history of not just the basketball program, but all of the athletic programs at KU. I found out that there were three Booth children: David, Mark, and Jane. The three of them had built the Hall of Athletics in memory of their late parents, Gilbert and Betty Booth.

"We literally grew up a stone's throw away, so the emotional component of this is hard to overstate," Mark Booth had said in a press release I found from the day they broke ground.

A stone's throw away . . . where did the Booths live? When I found the answer, I couldn't believe it. Gilbert and Betty Booth had raised their three children at 1931 Naismith Drive. I jumped on Google Maps to get a view of 1931 Naismith Drive and saw a tiny house, just steps away from Allen Fieldhouse. "Our parents had very few things they owned," continued Mark that day. "But one thing they owned was two tickets to the chair seats in Allen Fieldhouse."

The more I researched the Booth Family, the more impressed I became. The Booth boys, Mark and David, had left their humble home on Naismith Drive to essentially conquer the world. I learned that Mark had been incredibly successful in a variety of industries, serving as a CEO and chairman of famous companies in the US and abroad. Though a native of Kansas, it appeared from what I could make out that Mark now resided in England.

Luckily, it appeared that his brother, David, was based in the United States . . . and the more I learned about David, the more I realized that he was an absolute world-beater. Booth had earned both his bachelor's and master's degrees from the University of Kansas, before receiving his MBA from the University of Chicago. In 1981, David had founded an investment firm called Dimensional Fund Advisors, where he still served as chairman and chief executive officer. Dimensional had risen to become a leader in the industry by developing a reputation for successfully applying leading-edge academic research to money management. The firm managed a portfolio worth billions. It was quite evident that for my purposes, David Booth was a great place to start.

Then something else occurred to me: the Booth Family Hall of Athletics was far from the only building sitting on KU's campus named after a supportive and successful alumnus. I specifically recalled two other such buildings and quickly researched the men behind them. One was called the Horesji Family Athletics Center, which sat directly behind Allen Fieldhouse, and had been built with donations from KU alumnus Stewart Horesji. On the opposite side of campus was the Anderson Family Football Complex, donated by the family of KU grad Dana Anderson. Like Booth, both men had enjoyed successful business careers and made KU the prime target of their philanthropy. I knew that somehow, some way, I had to get to all three of these guys.

Wednesday, November 17: 23 Days Until Auction

I arrived to work the following morning with my three targets located, but was unsure of what to do next. How could I get in front of three complete strangers? Three leaders in their industry? Three extremely successful and busy men?

I decided with my three alumni targets in sight, that I wouldn't lie. I wouldn't tell them everything, but if I told them I was making a documentary—which I was—about KU basketball and James Naismith—which it was—then maybe I could get in front of them.

I put myself in their shoes. These were guys who undoubtedly got hit up for money at every turn. If I were to receive an unsolicited call from some stranger looking for a handout, I would surely be weary. I decided that I wouldn't tell them the real motive behind my visit until I saw them in person.

After a multitude of phone calls with liaisons and secretaries and executive assistants of assistants, I finally made it to Horesji and Anderson. Both men eventually agreed to meet with me. Anderson would be available the following week in Kansas, where he would be visiting family for Thanksgiving. Horesji would be available the day after that at his home in Paradise Valley, Arizona. David Booth was another matter altogether. His assistant said that he was in Fiji on a family vacation and that he wouldn't be back in the States until the end of the month, at which point he would be heading to Las Vegas for an executive conference. As luck would have it, the Kansas Jayhawks were scheduled to play in the Las Vegas Invitational just days before Booth's arrival. I decided we would hit Kansas for Anderson, head to Phoenix for Horesji, and then jaunt over to Las Vegas for the tournament and wait for Booth to arrive.

With the alumni maze coming together, I turned my attention to what I felt should be our first stop. I thought of Ian Naismith, the seller of the rules. I knew that he lived in a Chicago suburb and wondered how he would feel about the rules ending up at KU. When we met before, I had never even mentioned that I was a Kansas fan. In fact, I had never told Ian much of anything in regards to my motives. Now that I had one, as improbable as it appeared, it seemed that the right thing to do would be to share it with him.

Upon meeting Ian the week before, he had been quick to tell me that he was still recovering from the effects of a brutal stroke the year prior. So I dialed him again, unsure if he'd remember me . . . but he did. "Ian," I said. "I have something to tell you, but I can't do it over the phone. Would it be all right if I came to Chicago to see you?"

Ian kept the company of a close friend and consigliere named Mike LaChapelle, whose business card read: "Mike LaChapelle, Agent to the Rules."

"Mike saves me from myself," Ian had said half-jokingly the week before in New York. Mike was helping Ian manage all of the press demands surrounding the upcoming auction, and Ian did not book anything unless Mike could be there as well. I confirmed a meeting with both men for the upcoming Saturday at Ian's Illinois home.

With all that in place, there was still one final thing to explore. I considered the players who were currently playing on NBA rosters that had attended KU. I was about 20 percent convinced that this was a path worth pursuing. It wasn't that I doubted their love for Kansas basketball, but as public figures—especially ones so sought after securing such a contribution seemed like a stretch. Even if I could get in front of these guys, I doubted it was worth investing too much time.

I perused NBA schedules to see where I could efficiently work such stops into my schedule. Sure enough, the Milwaukee Bucks were hosting the Oklahoma City Thunder the Saturday we were supposed to meet Ian in Chicago. The Thunder had two former Jayhawks in Nick Collison and Cole Aldrich, and the Bucks had former Jayhawk great Drew Gooden. With the Bradley Center only an hour drive from Ian's home, it seemed like the perfect opportunity. I called my colleague, Jen Aiello, who had a long history of successfully booking athletes and talent, and explained to her what I was trying to do. I crafted an email that I hoped would pull at the heartstrings of the former Jayhawks and we sent it off to the PR contacts at Oklahoma City and Milwaukee.

In the meantime, I got comfortable with the game plan: first would be Ian in Chicago, followed by some NBA players in Milwaukee, followed by the three alumni meetings I had set up—all of which proved more than reason enough to go out on the road and at least give this a shot. I called Daymion to say we'd be leaving Saturday morning and that I was going to purchase us plane tickets. Daymion said that I needed to buy three, as he had found a second cameraman to join us on our quest.

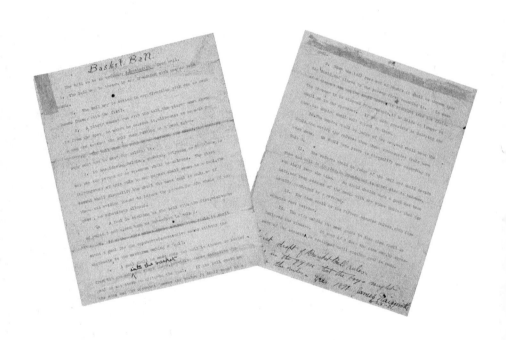

Basket Ball

3

MECCA

FROM THE MOMENT I set foot in Allen Fieldhouse as a kid, I knew what my future would hold. Once I had finished high school, I would spend four, five, perhaps even six years in Lawrence, engrossed in college basketball paradise. (Oh, and I'd attend a class or two.) This appeared to be the most logical path. Why wouldn't I go to KU? It had everything I could possibly want. I wasn't even thinking of post-college life or an inevitable ascension into the "real world." It never occurred to me that perhaps the University of Kansas was not the ideal destination for me. And why would it?

That was, of course, before puberty. And if puberty has a way of complicating youthful clarity, high school really can confuse things. It's as if suddenly, almost overnight, you are hyper-aware of yourself, your place in the world, and more importantly, your place in the school.

Upon entering high school, what became crystal clear to me was that my old identity wasn't going to work in this new world order. Suddenly no one wanted to huddle around and hear my thoughts on the Kansas basketball team. No one cared about my experience in the Fieldhouse the night before. This was no longer considered cool. I quickly realized what any moron could have: If I wanted to stay relevant, being the "crazy Jayhawk super fan" was not going to cut it anymore.

As I moved through high school, I began to consider my future. Not just college, but my future after graduation. I could almost see my own mundane existence around the corner, working in the family air conditioning business, getting scolded by my dad as I screwed up yet another cooling system. I decided that this wouldn't be me, that this couldn't be me. I began looking, searching for answers, for meaning in life.

During my senior year in high school, an answer came from the most unexpected place. I fell in love. Not with a girl (of this I was still terrified), but with music. Music for when I woke up; music for when I went to bed; music for when I was happy, thrilled to be alive. Music for when I was down, afraid of the future and all its uncertainty. This was of course not a revolutionary concept. For ages, teen angst had commonly been tempered by music.

I had been a DJ in high school. Could I make a living as a DJ, I wondered? That didn't exactly seem so appealing. But the music business did. The entertainment business did. Maybe I could work in the music industry and produce the records I so adored? Maybe I could produce TV shows or direct films? Perhaps Lawrence, Kansas, was not the most suitable college destination for me after all? I began to have doubts about KU. But it was too late. My fate was sealed. Tuition had been paid. There was simply no way I would be able to get out of going to the University of Kansas.

When I finally arrived at KU, the Jayhawks were coming off a Final Four appearance and remarkably had been to four of the previous eight Final Fours. Needless to say, excitement for Kansas basketball was at an all-time high. My excitement for KU, however, was at an all-time low. As I suspected, once I arrived to Lawrence, I felt lost. Somewhere between the film-school set and the die-hard basketball fan, I struggled to find my place among the sea of students at KU.

The super fan I had turned off in high school wasn't going back on, so when hoops season rolled around, I didn't wear a basketball over my head with two eyes cut out so I could see. I didn't paint my body crimson and blue. I didn't show up shirt-less in the dead of winter. Inconceivably, I didn't even sit in the student section I had once placed on the highest of pedestals.

Knowing full well what KU could have been, what it should have been, made my lack of bliss even more bothersome. Despite the overwhelming potential for a life filled with everything a warm-blooded young man could want: crazy parties, beau-tiful Midwestern girls, and consistent adolescent debauchery, I just couldn't get around one simple fact. It was all happening in Kansas. And I now wanted to get out of Dodge. Suddenly, college in Kansas seemed like time wasted to me. I was ready to set out on my own adventure, my own great quest of self-discovery. How could I do that in Kansas?

I suppose I would not have been so disgruntled with my locale had I not previously experienced—on multiple occasions—trips to the mecca of my existence. From a young age, my family and I had made several excursions to New York City to visit our extended family, and I fell in love with the city the minute I stepped into the taxi line at LaGuardia Airport. New York was like no movie I had ever seen. *People actually live here?* I remember thinking that first time we pulled into Manhattan, surrounded by enormous skyscrapers. Until that moment, I had assumed that everyone lived in the suburbs; the world seemed to be one giant subdivision of houses with lawns.

As I grew older and made consequent journeys to New York, my love for the city blossomed. Each trip on the subway, each excursion to the outer boroughs, every Manhattan back-alley and side-street felt strangely familiar, as if I had been there before.

Back at KU, I'd sit in the auditorium of the notorious flunk out course, Western Civ, and daydream about "Eastern Civ." I romanticized the New York of Jack Kerouac and the beat poets. I imagined the Greenwich Village of Bob Dylan at the dawn of folk music, The Factory of Andy Warhol and The Velvet Underground. I imagined CBGB's and The Ramones of the punk rock era, nights out at Studio 54 and Max's Kansas City. I wondered what scene was just around the corner? What cultural movement in New York would define my generation? With the new millennium approaching, I eagerly anticipated what was sure to be the greatest period of art and music, style, and culture that New York had ever known. I made up my mind. Somehow, some way, I needed to get to New York City.

Despite all my misery, at least I had Kansas basketball. When I attended games, it was still with my dad, and still in the same old seats up in the corner. Dad must have sensed something was wrong; I never even looked in the students' direction anymore.

We were extremely hopeful when March rolled around and Kansas was awarded a #1 seed in the 1995 NCAA Tournament.

The Jayhawks got by Colgate in Round One by a score of 82–68, and Western Kentucky in Round Two by a score of 75–70, to set up a Sweet Sixteen game with the fourth seed Virginia. We were convinced that another run to the Final Four was all but guaranteed. Getting past Virginia would just be a formality, nothing more than a game to play in and win. We were wrong. Kansas played awful and, much to our shock and disbelief, ended up losing, 67–58.

The loss to Virginia compounded my misery even more. I had been used to the Jayhawks softening life's blows. I could be confused, depressed, and frustrated, but at least I had Kansas basketball to fall back on. (When thing are going good in life, a tough loss is much easier to handle. When things are going bad, a tough loss is gut wrenching. Your entire world and all your supposed problems are magnified times a hundred. Everything seems to be collapsing around you. The world is a cold, harsh, unforgiving place during these times.)

This loss also marked the return of a thought that had first reared its ugly head two years prior after a similarly excruciating loss to UTEP—a thought that went something like this: "Perhaps I am the biggest loser on the face of the earth. Perhaps the fact that year after year I put all of my happiness into the outcome of a basketball game that I have no control over is just plain idiotic. Perhaps I need to get a life." After losing to Virginia, I started to think there was some real truth to this thought and became determined to do something about it.

When the school year ended and summer finally began, I was summoned to my father's sheet metal shop, being groomed to one day join the family business. Little did he or anyone else know that I had applied and been accepted to attend the City

University of New York (CUNY). And if I hoped to enroll in school that following fall, I was running out of time to make it known. More specifically, since I wasn't financially self-sufficient, I was running out of time to ask my parents for permission.

I rehearsed it over and over in my mind. I practiced an elaborate explanation as to why this was not only what I wanted to do, but also the right thing to do. I would explain how I had carefully chosen to attend a public school that would cost the same as KU. I would explain how I would get a job and pay for any cost of living differences between the two. I would explain how having my aunt, uncle, and cousins in nearby Long Island would offer a safe haven when the city proved too much. I memorized rebuttals to combat every conceivable reason they could think of saying no. I prepared like a seasoned courtroom attorney whose client's life hung in the balance. Written notes here, Post-It notes there. I prepared harder for this great exposition than I had for the sum of all my freshman tests. And when I could no longer wait to unleash my great dissertation, my closing argument for the ages, I opened my mouth to begin.

But nothing came out.

Except tears. Tears raced out of me. All the frustration, all the year's confusion. Everything I thought this period of my life would be but wasn't. The pressure of delivering an award-winning speech at that very moment. The disappointing Jayhawks. All the missed free throws through the years. All the underachieving star recruits. All the number one seeds with nothing to show for it. All of it came crashing down . . . on my face.

My parents had no choice but to let me go.

I would miss Kansas basketball. I would miss Allen Fieldhouse, the old barn that had served as a marking point of my youth. Some people had pictures, but I had games. At ten, I watched a freshman named Danny Manning launch a legendary career. At fifteen, I watched as Kansas beat a Rick Pitino–coached Kentucky Wildcats team by 55 points. Just the year before I'd seen Jacque Vaughn hit a buzzer-beating three in overtime to defeat Bobby Knight and the Indiana Hoosiers. It would be hard to leave the program, to give up that seat next to my dad. But it was time for my younger brother to finally realize the uninterrupted, season-long experience that I had enjoyed for so long. It was his turn to reign supreme in the grade school lunchroom, recalling the scenes from last night's game, an audience of jealous kids hanging on his every word.

Surely I could catch the big games on TV. But partially I was leaving to get away from Kansas basketball. It had recently become clear that I was not healthy. And I thought that maybe, just maybe, I wouldn't need Kansas basketball anymore. Perhaps I would be so fulfilled in New York that it would no longer be so important in my life.

I kissed my mom and my siblings. I petted my dog. I hugged my friends. Then I turned to face my dad. Never one to care for the big city, he didn't understand why I was leaving in the first place. "Why would you want to leave when you have everything you need here?" he seemed to say without actually saying it. I think he was upset to be losing a third of the fan unit he had worked so hard to create. I suppose if it were up to him, we'd be together watching every game until I'd eventually bring my son from down the street as we built our Jayhawk army one by one. But mostly he was sad because I think deep down he knew I was gone and never coming back.

The Journey

Saturday, November 20: 20 Days Until Auction

Avi met us at LaGuardia Airport to catch our flight for Chicago. Avi worked for an equipment rental house in the city called Scheimpflug, where Daymion rented all of his photography equipment. Daymion had shown up to Scheimpflug days before in a panic, unsure of what he needed to shoot a film. The shop owner, John, a close friend of Daymion's, pressed him on his unusual predicament. When Daymion confided his fears about shooting moving images as well as the audio that accompanied it, John considered Daymion's dilemma. John queried Daymion on the details of the film and immediately became enthralled with the story.

John then offered the services of his new hire, Avi, a man skilled in all facets of film and sound. John was certain that Avi would be the perfect solution for Daymion out on the road. On the strength of his friendship with Daymion, without having ever met me, without having ever witnessed a game in Allen Fieldhouse, John pledged Avi and all of the necessary equipment to the project for a price that would fit nicely into our budget: free.

Arriving at Chicago's O'Hare Airport, we jumped into a rental car and began the forty-five-minute drive to Ian's suburban home. When we finally pulled into his driveway, I felt a range of emotions. I was excited to be chasing a dream—as impossible as it seemed—but I was unsure of how Ian would react. In New York, Ian had mentioned he'd like to see the rules at the Smithsonian. I wondered how Ian felt about the University of Kansas?

Years before the rules went on auction, it had been well documented that the Naismith family as a whole felt estranged from KU, the institution so beloved by James Naismith that he famously said in a commencement speech, "I have loved three things in my life: God, my family, and the University of Kansas."

For decades, the Naismiths felt their family patriarch had never received his just due from the university. Considering the Kansas Jayhawks play basketball in a building not named for the game's inventor, one can't help but sympathize with their position. It wasn't until 1997, over forty years after Allen Fieldhouse opened its doors, that the court was named "James Naismith Court." To many in the Naismith clan, that was too little too late.

Upon entering Ian's house, it was clear that we had found him at a time of transition. As he would explain, his wife Renee had passed away a few years prior, and he no longer wished to stay in the house the two had called home.

Ian was headed for the Outer Banks of North Carolina to seemingly get away from it all. But before he did, there was one last order of business to tend to: the selling of the rules. Packing a life's worth of belongings had been a work in progress. Overstuffed boxes filled the space, spilling from one room to the next. A back bedroom doubled as the foundation's headquarters and housed a slew of pictures and tutorials that made up the information packets Ian would take with him on the road for his Naismith Sportsmanship Tour stops. In every nook and cranny of the house was another accoutrement from Ian's life in basketball's periphery: an autographed ball here, a signed poster there, pictures of Ian and some esteemed hoops legend everywhere.

Ian's right hand man, Mike LaChapelle, was waiting for us with him. After greeting the two and taking a quick tour around the place, we settled into Ian's office. There, on Ian's desk, sat the infamous gold briefcase that he had carted the rules around in for years. As we made small talk while Daymion and Avi finished setting up, I could sense that Ian and Mike were very curious as to why I had decided that on a Saturday afternoon, some twenty days before the auction, I absolutely needed to see them.

I started with the basics: "I'm a Kansas fan," I said.

"As I am too," said Ian.

"You are?"

"Yes. I started school there," he said. "I finished at Texas A&M, but I started at the University of Kansas."

My anxiety began to dissolve a bit. "Well that's great. Then maybe you'll be into what I'm doing. I'm going out and I'm trying to raise money, to bring the rules back to Lawrence. And that's why I had to come here today, to tell you that in person."

Ian looked relieved. "Here it was I thought you were coming to tell me you were my long lost son," he said half-joking. Ian thought about it some more and then got serious. "There's a saying in the Naismith family that basketball was born in Massachusetts but was raised in Kansas. And that's a saying that's been around a long time. With the Naismith legend, you can't separate the two . . . nor do we try. It's fascinating how powerful that game is there in Kansas," he said.

"What would it mean for the rules to end up in Lawrence?" I asked.

"Well, it'd be full circle. I mean he was there forty-one years. We're part of that legacy. And I think for the rules to end up in Lawrence would be absolutely the proper place."

Ian's endorsement was music to my ears. I was not expecting him to be so agreeable. I was thrilled to have his support but, more importantly, I was comforted by his concurrence that Lawrence was a suitable destination. I would never have wanted to embark on a mission that went against the wishes of the Naismith family, and now that I had their blessing, I felt I could move forward with a clear conscience. Perhaps Ian got caught up in the moment, perhaps he appreciated the fact that I'd come all this way to pay him my respect and ask for the family's blessing. Either way, I was surprised by what he said next.

"I gotta tell ya, Josh. I'm very proud of you and I don't hardly know you. Because you just took up the Naismith call in a big way, son. And that does good by Naismith people. So, welcome to the family. Welcome to the family because you're doing it from the heart."

"I'm doing it because I love KU," I said.

"You love KU and you love the game."

"I love the game," I said.

"So now you've got the torch as far as the University of Kansas goes," he said. As we left Ian's, he handed us a picture of his grandfather standing atop Mount Oread, carrying a peach basket and a ball. "Here," said Ian. "May he guide you on your journey."

It felt surreal standing courtside at the Bradley Center watching Drew Gooden go through one-on-one drills. Gooden had been a star at KU for three years. Following a run to the Final Four his junior year, Gooden left Kansas for the NBA. Since his arrival in the league, however, it had been tough for him to find a place to call home, having played on a total of nine different teams. But before the season began, Gooden agreed to a 5 year, $32 million contract with the Milwaukee Bucks. It seemed that he had finally found a home in the NBA.

As we waited with the Bucks PR assistant, tremendous anxiety flooded my mind as a slew of questions arose. Was Kansas still important to him? Did he even care about James Naismith and the original rules? Would he find this all ridiculous? Was it, indeed, ridiculous? Was I just wasting everyone's time? Would I keep my nerve? (I'd never interviewed an athlete before, let alone courtside before an NBA game.) And last but not least, could I actually get up the nerve to ask him for money? Tracking down wealthy donors was one thing, but cornering a pro athlete with a camera in his face, at his place of work nonetheless, was another altogether.

Gooden finally made his way to where I was standing. Right away, his enormous smile put me at ease. When he held out his hand, it was clear that he was ready to talk KU. I decided to ease into it and begin by learning about how he arrived in Kansas in the first place.

"Well, I'm from California and I went on a trip to Kansas and had never been to the state before," said Gooden. "What stood out to me was the tradition. I never knew that basketball had basically originated in Kansas. So, it was special to me. But it was tough for me to leave California. I had to leave my family and it wasn't an easy transition, especially since I was seventeen, but I eventually adjusted and it became home."

I knew Gooden was aware of the upcoming auction because we had discussed it briefly before the interview had officially begun. So I asked him what it would mean to have Naismith's rules in Allen Fieldhouse.

"Well, playing in Allen Fieldhouse is just unexplainable. There is nothing like the atmosphere in that building on game day. So I think it would be great for the school and the city of Lawrence, and the history of Kansas basketball to have those official rules from 1891 in that building. I know Springfield, Massachusetts is a popular site for Naismith, but at the end of the day, the fans at KU deserve to have those rules."

Gooden had teed it up perfectly and I felt if I was going to ask him the hard question I better do it now. "These rules are going to be expensive," I said. "What I'm doing is going across the country to talk to anyone and everyone who might be in a position to help us win this thing. Do you want to help us out?"

Gooden smiled before answering. "I mean, the official rules aren't really something you can get on eBay now, are they? I'll tell you what, get in touch with me and we'll see what we can make happen."

Though he politely sidestepped my question, he did seem very taken by my mission. "Thank you Josh," he said as we wrapped up. "I really want to thank you for doing this." While I wasn't sure if Drew was a viable candidate for securing money, I could feel the wholehearted sincerity in his well wishes.

Former Jayhawk big man and Oklahoma City Thunder rookie Cole Aldrich was practicing on the other end of the court along with Nick Collison, another former Jayhawk. The Thunder's team policy forbid players suiting up from fulfilling any sort of media, film, or television requests during road games. As such, we were not allowed to meet with Collison. But because Aldrich was only a rookie, and unlikely to get in the game much, we were given permission to meet with him courtside.

Like Gooden, Aldrich had also left KU after his junior season. Now as a rookie in the NBA, perhaps he could reflect on his time in Kansas with some healthy separation.

"What is it about Kansas that you fell in love with?" I asked him.

"Well, there's so much," he said. "It's the fans, the atmosphere, just everything really. You know, it's a very special place."

"Where do you think Naismith's original rules should be?" I pressed.

"Well I think there are many places that the rules could be, but I think there's, there's only one place that the rules should be. They should be in Allen Fieldhouse just because, I mean, you got a guy that created basketball and then that's where it all started. I mean that's pretty much the birthplace of basketball is, is in Lawrence."

"So that brings me to what I'm doing," I said. "I'm trying to raise money to go to the auction and win these rules for KU. What do you think? We're building a pot here. Would you be interested in contributing?"

"Yeah, I'll definitely donate some money in there," he replied. "I think it would really be special, you know, just to have that there."

After finishing up with Cole, I settled in to watch the game and reflect on what had transpired. I felt touched by Cole and Drew's willingness to hear from me further and considered the possible next steps. Perhaps I'd reach out to their agents? Or maybe I'd follow up with their PR folks or their lawyers? Anyway I sliced it, it seemed that there would be some sort of middleman involved. It was clear how much these guys loved the Kansas program and my sense was all NBA players from KU still felt that same connection. But, at the same time, I knew in my heart of hearts that they were not the answer. To actually get money from them would surely involve an endless series of meetings with some type of agent, accountant, attorney, or confidant—and more than likely all of the above. And I simply didn't have time for that. I decided to turn my attention to Kansas, where I would be meeting with my first big alumnus.

Sunday, November 21: 19 Days Until Auction

My parents were away, so once arriving in Kansas, we pulled into my grandmother's home inside a retirement community. Her central location in Overland Park, a suburb of Kansas City, would prove ideal. When she pressed me for the reason behind my surprise visit, I tried as best as I could to explain to her just exactly what I was trying to do. But every time I attempted to do so, I could hear myself sounding ridiculous. "Basketball rules. Auction. Millions. Jayhawks. Naismith."

When my grandmother gave me a look that only a grandmother can give, I began to second-guess myself. I wondered if I was finally taking my Kansas basketball obsession too far. I decided that I needed some spiritual guidance. Since my grandmother lived next door to the synagogue, I decided to mosey on over and see if I could get some.

It felt like I hadn't set foot in Congregation B'Nai Jehudah for well over twenty years, not since my bar mitzvah at least. So now, as I sat down with Rabbi Nemitoff, some twenty-two years later, I was hoping he'd help me find my way.

I explained to the rabbi my mission, what I was trying to do with Naismith and the rules of basketball. And then I asked him if he thought perhaps I was on the wrong path in life. If in fact I was putting far too much importance on something that would seem trivial to many? He thought about it carefully before responding.

"It's a problem if you are so obsessed that you lose your sense of balance in life," he finally said.

I have definitely lost a sense of balance, I thought.

"If it becomes the overarching cause in your life, then it's problematic," he added.

I thought about this for a moment. Kansas basketball had long indeed been the overarching cause in my life. It seemed the rabbi was onto something. He was confirming my fear. Perhaps this had all been a giant mistake. I was ready to thank him for setting me straight, for putting me back on the path of adulthood and responsibility, rationality, and maturity. But before I could, the rabbi continued.

"But your experiences in Kansas, being part of the Jayhawk faithful, is an important part of who you are."

Wait, what's this?

"When we are steeped in a tradition, it gives us a sense of being centered. A sense of knowing who we are and what our place is in the world. And these rules, if you are successful and you are able to bring them back, back to KU, back to Lawrence, it would be a wonderful culmination of taking the past, and what you hope to be a wonderful future for KU," he said.

Rabbi Nemitov was on fire.

"There is, I believe within our tradition, the notion that when we find something that gives us meaning in our lives, we need to hold on to it, we need to nurture it, we need to encourage it. If we're doing it for noble causes, for good causes, then our tradition says it will be a task that is well received, and a task that will be fulfilled. And so I challenge you, Josh. May your cause be noble. May your intent be noble and may your efforts be successful, if in the end, it improves the lives of those who surround you."

And with that, I had experienced the single greatest sermon of my life. Yes, my cause was noble! Yes, I would go in peace and come back in peace and just . . . be peaceful! I was ready to burst out of the rabbi's office and get these rules.

"Wait," said the rabbi.

Oy, I thought. Here comes the reality check.

Rabbi Nemitov picked up the phone on his desk. He looked through his Rolodex and began to dial. "One of our members is a huge Jayhawk fan," he said. "He might be into this. Let me see if I can get you a meeting."

When the rabbi told his friend the expected sale price, a meeting seemed unlikely. Still, I floated out of the synagogue on a religious high. This truly had been the single greatest trip to temple in my life.

Daymion, Avi, and I got cleaned up and headed downtown to Kansas City. As luck would have it, the College Basketball Hall of Fame, located in Kansas City, was having its annual induction ceremony and, on this night, former basketball luminaries would be enshrined, including Jerry West, David Thompson, Sidney Wicks, and former Duke great Christian Laettner. The entire Duke team would be in attendance to support Laettner, since they were also playing in a tournament at the Sprint Center just next door. I was interested in scoping out the Duke program to see if I could sniff a scent of their interest in the rules.

On my first trip to Sotheby's, I was informed that they had heard from people with interest in the rules that represented universities with "strong basketball programs." Of everything I had heard that first day, all the testament to the rules and their profound importance in the pantheon of world sport, not one statement had affected me as greatly as the notion that *other schools wanted the rules.* It would be one thing for KU not to get the rules and for them to end up in the hands of a private collector, and it would be another thing entirely for them to end up at the Smithsonian or the Basketball Hall of Fame and not at KU. But I *could not* live in a world where the rules of basketball lived at another university, especially one we engaged in heated recruiting battles with, and raced with for wins, legacy, and tradition.

Leaving the auction house that day, I went through the list of the big five in my head. I knew where Kansas stood: They had no plan and no intentions of hatching one. UCLA seemed implausible. Just the year prior I had gone to a decrepit Pauley Pavilion to see KU handily beat UCLA. I was shocked to find a lethargic crowd half-full of Kansas fans. While the media desperately clung to the heyday of John Wooden, the UCLA fan base seemed almost uninterested in basketball. *They certainly weren't putting together a plan for Naismith's original rules,* I thought.

Kentucky seemed like less of a long shot. The basketball fanatics that comprise the passionate bluegrass fan base think they all but invented the game of basketball. James Naismith had mentored their most famous coach, Adolph Rupp, at Kansas, so it didn't seem out of the question for them to have interest. Perhaps the rules were just what Rupp Arena needed to put it more solidly in the conversation as the best venue in college hoops.

I thought of North Carolina. Ever since Michael Jordan had graced the floor at the Dean Smith Center, Chapel Hill had long been a hotbed of hoops hysteria. Like Rupp at Kentucky, Carolina's famous coach, Dean Smith, had roots tracing back to Kansas and Naismith as well. Carolina making a push for the rules—while a stretch—seemed reasonable enough.

Then there was Duke University, the private school sitting just seven miles down Tobacco Road from UNC. Duke had emerged over the last quarter century as college basketball royalty. Compared to the other four public school institutions comprising college basketball's "blue-bloods," Duke was a private school known for academics. If any school had a long list of affluent alumni who could afford the rules, it would be Duke.

With the advent of ESPN and NCAA tournament expansion, no brand had become bigger than Duke basketball. It seemed like every time you turned on ESPN there was another Duke home game with Dick Vitale himmering and hollering about the Dukies and how special their players and fans were. Behind head coach Mike Krzyzewski, Cameron Indoor Stadium had become a college hoops fortress, often mentioned atop the bucket lists of analysts and hoops aficionados alike . . . just like Allen Fieldhouse.

When we arrived at the event, we had no press credentials waiting for us—which was to be expected, as we had made no prior arrangements. But since I was accompanied by two guys holding cameras, they quickly let me in, thinking it had been a simple oversight on their end, which I assured them it had been. Festivities were well underway with a panel of esteemed inductees perched onstage. Emceeing the ceremony was Seth Davis, the college basketball analyst from CBS and *Sports Illustrated.*

As the Duke team roamed the interactive exhibits, I decided to try and get their thoughts on the rules. I harassed players like the Plumlee Twins (Miles and Mason), Andre Dawkins, Kyrie Irving, and Seth Curry. While some entertained my questions, most of them brushed me off. Because of the media swarm around him, I couldn't quite reach Coach K, so I tracked down Duke assistant coach Steve Wojciechowski. "Wojo" thought the rules belonged at the Hall of Fame in Springfield.

The last Dukie I approached didn't play basketball, but he knew the game as well as anyone on the planet. Seth Davis couldn't help but pursue a career in college basketball. Having graduated from Duke University in 1992, Davis witnessed Duke basketball become "Duke basketball." Davis was a student during Duke's first National Championship in 1991 and saw them repeat in 1992. I asked Davis what he thought of the rules.

"Well it's almost like inheriting the Torah, its hallowed ground. It's a holy document, that has spurred a great and wonderful game," he said.

"I'm trying to get these rules back to Kansas," I said. "What do you think of that?"

"Well, it doesn't surprise me," he said.

"Why is that?" I pressed.

"Well, for a Kansas fan to take on a mission such as this is fitting because I truly believe that Kansas has the best fans in all of college basketball."

"Wait, what was that?" I asked him again, thinking I had misunderstood.

"I think Kansas has the best fans in college basketball," Davis said again. "So it doesn't surprise me that you are leading the charge for the rules. Kansas fans really appreciate the history of their university. You have Naismith's name on the court, you have Phog Allen's name on the building. I think it would be incredibly appropriate for the rules to end up at Kansas. After all, there's only one school that had James Naismith as a coach . . . and he started it all."

I left the event thinking Duke people were much smarter than I thought.

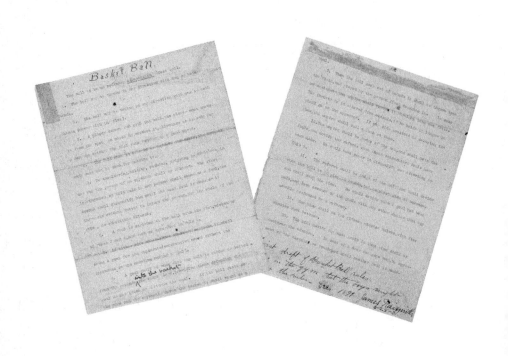

4

NOT IN KANSAS ANYMORE

I ARRIVED IN NEW York City with all the hopefulness that
accompanies most transplants arriving to the Big Apple in
search of a new life. But still, I wasn't ready to leave Kansas
completely behind. I decided that if I had any hope of surviving
in the big city I had to locate some fellow Jayhawk fans to watch
games with. (Locating such a group was not a remedial task
before the Internet made finding things like KU fans in New
York City as easy as the click of a mouse.)

Things began to take a turn for the better when a random
lead from a friend back home materialized into something real.
This friend had heard from his older sister whose friend lived in
New York that the NY chapter of the KU Alumni Association
gathered to have watch parties at a place called the Park Avenue
Country Club. My friend had relayed this information to me
just after the season began, but I did nothing about it.

I had no desire to check out this Country Club place. I imagined the New York chapter of the KU Alumni Association to be

comprised of boring yuppie-types, with whom I had nothing in common. On top of that, their gathering place of choice having the words "Country Club" in the title made the whole thing sound as appealing as a continuing education class.

But when conference play ended I turned desperate. Kansas marched to a conference title and with the NCAA Tournament about to begin, I stumbled into the Country Club thinking it would in fact be the lamest Kansas watch-party I'd ever witnessed. But it wasn't. Much to my delight, I was astonished to find Kansas fans everywhere. These were not boring old posers in sweater vests sipping espresso. These were real die-hards like me. Turns out, I wasn't the first person to escape the Kansas suburbs for the bright lights of New York.

Kansas entered the NCAA Tournament as a #2 seed, and held serve making it all the way to the Elite Eight for a matchup with the 4th seeded Syracuse Orangemen. I arrived at the Park Avenue Country Club to find a bar full of both Kansas and Syracuse fans. Whereas the Country Club was the city's designated Kansas bar, with so many Syracuse alumni in the city, almost every sports bar was designated for the Orangemen as well. So to find that they too had laid claim to the Country Club was not surprising in the least.

As tip-off grew closer, a back-and-forth squabble erupted between the Kansas and Syracuse contingencies. The arguing seemed to in some way involve some variation of the following: Kansas fans projecting an air of superiority over the Syracuse basketball program, leaving the Syracuse fans no choice but to point out, as if it was the funniest thing in the world, "You're from Kansas."

A game of runs came down to one final possession. The Jayhawks trailed by 3 points as time wound down. When KU's Jacque Vaughn missed a tying 3-point shot, the game was over. The Syracuse players jumped up and down and their fans gathered at the Park Avenue Country Club did the same. Caught in the eye of the Syracuse celebration, I tried my best to drown out the "Final Four" chants that had begun to ring in unison. I put my head down and fought through the locals deep in celebration. Once I finally reached the door, one last Syracuse fan whispered in my ear as if he really meant to separate this insult from the other anti-Kansas sentiment flailing about, "You're not in Kansas anymore."

Back in my tiny dorm room, it occurred to me just how right my dad had been. He'd been right about the big city in all of its self-aggrandizing glory. He'd been right about New Yorkers who struggled to imagine a world existing outside the tri-state area. And he'd been right about something else . . . something he'd been ranting about my entire life . . . something called "East Coast bias."

East Coast bias is a long-standing notion in sports that because the East Coast serves as the major media hub in America, networks, papers, and the so-called experts they employ place more emphasis on East Coast events while more prominently featuring games, teams, and players who play in their time zone. The backlash against East Coast bias is aimed at these same national media figures who seemingly place on a pedestal the teams nearest to their locale.

No one leads the charge against East Coast bias like KU fans. To die-hard Jayhawk fans, Kansas basketball is a national treasure ingrained deep into the fabric of American sports, a narrative of the highest order. It is a legacy passed down from grandfathers to fathers to sons to babies swaddled in Jayhawk onesies. This was basketball's greatest tradition by a landslide. But where was the national reverence? We were confused as to why the Atlantic Coast Conference and Big East dominated the national headlines. But we were mostly confused as to how so-called professionals who made a living as sports commentators could so frequently forget about a program so entangled in the history of a sport that was so entangled into the fiber of America.

Before coming to New York, I had never really bought into the East Coast bias conjecture circulating inside my home. Didn't KU receive its fair share of love from the national media? Weren't the Jayhawks always on ESPN? Wasn't Allen Fieldhouse always mentioned as one of the best college arenas in the country? Besides, the simple truth was, we kept choking when it mattered . . . in the tournament, like we had again this year. But now that I had spent a season in New York living amongst the East Coast sportswriters (and fans), I was starting to believe in the conspiracy theory. Watching games surrounded by Syracuse, UConn, and New York basketball fans who came out of the womb being told their entire East Coast life was the end all be all of creation had proved to be nothing short of maddening.

I wondered, *Do these people really not grasp the roots of a game they have claimed as their divine right? Do they actually believe that "New York City is the mecca of basketball* as I had heard time and again since my arrival?

The entire thing had proved infuriating because if I knew anything, I knew this: Kansas may not have had 200 city blocks or Madison Square Garden or the Metropolitan Museum of Art, but damn it, if we had anything, we had basketball. And the mecca . . . the "spiritual center" of the game, was in fact not New York City, but rather a sleepy college town in the middle of the United States where the game's creator rests for eternity.

5

GENESIS

JAMES NAISMITH WAS born November 6, 1861, the second of three children to John and Margaret in the rural town of Ramsey in Ontario, Canada. He endured a difficult childhood, tragically losing both parents to typhoid fever when he was only nine years old. Religion, specifically Christianity, became the guiding force in his life and at an early age Naismith set his sights on a career in the ministry.

While in college, Naismith became enthralled with organized gatherings of another kind: athletics. He realized that it took many of the same qualities to become a good athlete as it did to become a good Christian, including enthusiasm, perseverance, and hard work. His epiphany had come on the heels of a growing movement called "Muscular Christianity," which preached the spiritual value of sports, especially those involving a team working towards a singular goal.

Naismith's love for sports grew so strong that he had second thoughts on pursuing the pulpit and eventually decided to pursue a career in athletics. He enrolled at the YMCA Training

College in Springfield, Massachusetts—the first school of its kind, dedicated to preparing young men for careers in the field. Upon arriving at the training school, Naismith was pleased to meet another Muscular Christian also enrolled named Amos Alonzo Stagg. Stagg had been a star football and baseball player at Yale, as well as a theology student. Both Naismith and Stagg had ultimately chosen careers in athletics over the ministry. At Springfield, they began a close friendship that would last the rest of their lives.

Foreshadowing the tremendous success each would have in their respective careers, Naismith and Stagg completed the two-year course at Springfield in just one year. Afterwards, both were asked to remain the following year as members of the faculty. In their first year as staff members, they launched a Springfield football team to a great degree of success. But once the harshness of winter set in, there was little in the way of organized athletics available to the young men in both Springfield and beyond. Baseball and track took place in the warm months and the students quickly became bored with the gymnastics and calisthenics performed in the gymnasium when it was too cold outside to play. The Springfield teachers were aware of the growing unease amongst the students, but none of them had any idea how to solve the problem.

"We needed some sort of game that would be interesting and could be played indoors," Naismith recalled. "We had a seminar where we discussed those things quite frequently. During one such meeting, Dr. Gulick (Naismith's mentor at Springfield), made this statement: "There's nothing new under the sun, but all new things are simply a re-combination of the factors of existing things." Gulick wanted "a competitive game—like football or lacrosse—but it must be a game that can be played indoors. It must be a game requiring skill and sportsmanship, providing exercise for the whole body, and yet must be one that can be played without extreme roughness or damage to the players and equipment."

"We can go to work to invent a new game," Naismith immediately replied to Gulick, a statement he would soon regret when Gulick put the task of developing such a game solely on his shoulders. Naismith took to the mission, racking his brain, consulting with others in the field, and seeking out input wherever he could.

Naismith's hand was soon forced when two very capable teachers quit one class of eighteen secretarial students who had rebelled against the calisthenic-oriented instruction that dominated the course. Failing to arouse any enthusiasm, the two previous teachers had walked out and given up on the "incorrigibles." Gullick assigned Naismith to the class to see if he could keep this rebellious group engaged. "Now would be a good time for you to work on that new game you said could be invented," said Gullick, and he gave Naismith two weeks to come up with an idea. "My fate was sealed," Naismith recalled.

Naismith pushed the deadline to the last day, racking his brain to come up with an idea that would satisfy both his boss and his class of restless students. On the night before his deadline, Naismith came up with the rules for a new game that would soon be called "Basket Ball." (The name of the game would eventually be changed to one word: "basketball.") Naismith would later say that from the minute he threw up that first jump ball, he knew he was onto something.

Basketball was an instant hit with the young men at the YMCA. A few months later a group of Springfield girls got in on the action by participating in the first women's basketball tournament in history. Playing that day was a pretty girl named Maude Sherman. Naismith had long been smitten with Maude, who happened to be the daughter of his landlady. After meeting on the court, James and Maude began their courtship. In June of 1894, they were married at the Hope Congregational Church in Springfield, where they lived for one year as a married couple.

As the game of basketball began to travel throughout the growing network of YMCAs, James and his new wife set their sights on doing the same. Highly thought of at the Training College, Naismith could have remained a member of the Springfield faculty for as long as he wanted. But like his mentor Dr. Gulick, Naismith wanted a medical degree. He had always been interested in medicine, and patching up various injuries in the gymnasium through the years had only increased his desire to gain proper training. As Maude and James welcomed baby daughter Margaret into the world in July of 1895, Naismith knew a medical degree would not only further his career, but also provide financial stability for his young family. James knew he needed to find a medical school in close proximity to a YMCA, where he'd be sure to land another job.

In the summer of 1895, Naismith found such a chance when he was offered a position as the director of physical education at the YMCA in Denver, Colorado. The Denver YMCA was the biggest in North America and it happened to be close to a respected medical school. Naismith accepted the job and was admitted to the Gross Medical School (now known as the University of Colorado School of Medicine). Along with his young daughter and wife, he set out west for a new home in the Rocky Mountains.

In addition to his new job overseeing physical education at the largest Y in America, Naismith continued his medical schooling. Thirty-four years old and a freshman once again, Naismith wasted no time jumping into a full course load. Balancing such a schedule would be too much for most, but Naismith, a man defined by his workmanship, forged ahead, focused on the task at hand.

Naismith and Maude gave birth to their second daughter, Helen, on December 21, 1897, six years to the date since Naismith had introduced basketball at the Springfield Y. Soon after, Naismith graduated with his medical degree and was ready for a new professional challenge.

In the meantime, Naismith's old friend, Amos Alonzo Stagg, had taken a job as the physical education director and football coach at the University of Chicago. Stagg and Naismith had remained in touch, and Stagg was aware of Naismith's recent graduation from medical school and his readiness for a new challenge. Stagg got a message one day from his boss, William Harper, the president of the University of Chicago. Harper's counterpart at the University of Kansas, Francis Snow, had contacted Harper to see if he could make a recommendation for a new position Kansas had created. The new position required a chapel leader to conduct daily prayers on campus and someone to head up the Department of Physical Education.

When hearing the details of the job Kansas was trying to fill, Stagg had no hesitation in making his recommendation. He fired off a telegram to Snow that read, "Recommend James Naismith, inventor of basketball, medical doctor, Presbyterian

Minister, tee-totaler, all-around athlete, non smoker, and owner of a vocabulary without cuss words. Address Y.M.C.A., Denver, Colorado."

It was only a matter of time before Kansas officials contacted Naismith and offered him the position, which he accepted. Nowhere in his job description did the term "basketball coach" appear, as Kansas University did not have a basketball team. While basketball was growing in popularity, no one at that time seemed to care who invented it. Naismith claimed that the only reason he was offered the job at KU was because he knew how to pray.

James, Maude, and their family settled into a house at 1219 Tennessee Street in Lawrence, Kansas. At KU, Naismith began teaching the mandatory freshman class in hygiene as well as the gymnastics classes. This was in addition to his primary responsibility to lead the daily chapel service, which he did to much success.

Success was harder to come by in athletics however. Upon his arrival, Naismith had found the KU athletic department to be basically nonexistent. So he decided to introduce basketball at the university, hoping it would jumpstart the athletic program and build interest in sports as a whole.

Naismith organized eight teams that began competing against one another on campus. After a few months, the most eager basketball students were hungry for competition beyond intramural, so Naismith organized a match up against the Kansas City YMCA. On February 4, 1899, KU played its first ever game, a 16–5 loss in Kansas City. The following week, KU played its first home game at the Lawrence Skating Rink, defeating the Topeka branch of the YMCA, 31–6. Kansas would go on to finish that first year with a 7–4 record. Unfortunately for Coach Naismith, winning seasons would prove hard to come by in Lawrence. But it was not a sign of things to come.

Over the course of his nine years at the helm, Naismith's Jayhawk teams compiled a record of 55 wins versus 60 losses. Seven coaches later, he remains the only losing coach in Kansas basketball history, a distinction that has followed him to the grave. But it's a distinction that is not really fair. Though the history books refer to James Naismith as the first basketball coach at KU, the fact of the matter is he was never hired to fill such a position and instead spent most games acting as an impartial referee, ensuring that the rules of the game were strictly adhered to.

Winning and losing aside, basketball had been just the spark Naismith hoped it would be. Around the new sport, KU's athletic department had begun to take shape. Said the *Kansas University Weekly*, "A new game has sprung into popularity. It is the game of basketball. It is talked at the club; it is discussed in the corridors; it is practiced and played in the gymnasium and on the campus. At present, it appears that the basketball mania would carry all before it."

It would carry all after it as well. In 115 years since Naismith introduced the game in Lawrence, Kansas's love affair with basketball has ceased to extinguish in the least.

6

THE SON

IF JAMES NAISMITH, the creator, was a sort-of metaphorical God to us Kansas fans, then when honoring the legacy of one Forrest Clare Allen, the Christian definition of Jesus seems fitting. For here was a man that too had an all-powerful, one-word name: "Phog." This was a name with inherent weight worthy of the highest order of praise from generations of faithful followers. Miraculously, Phog would become bigger and more integral to the game of basketball than the man who had actually invented the game.

Growing up, Forrest Allen and his five brothers loved to play games and spent heaps of time in the backyard engaged in a variety of different sports. To assemble enough players for baseball meant they had no choice but to recruit other neighborhood boys to join in. (Forrest earned the nickname "Foghorn" umpiring those backyard baseball games, yelling out the word *ball* in a foghorn voice. Foghorn was later shortened to "Fog" and years later when a reporter changed the spelling to "Phog" because it was more "interesting," the name stuck.)

As the sport of basketball grew more popular in the late 1890s, the six Allen brothers had found a game in which together they formed the perfect team, with a substitute to boot. It was the oldest brother, the very gifted Pete Allen, who piqued the other boy's interest in basketball when he first joined the Independence, Missouri, YMCA team. In 1899 Forrest sat in a hayloft barn and watched two of the first organized basketball games to ever be played when Pete's YMCA team took on the Jayhawks from Kansas. The games were officiated by none other than James Naismith, the newly appointed physical education director at KU.

While Pete went on to play football at the University of Kansas, Forrest joined the Blue Diamonds of the Kansas City Athletic Club in downtown Kansas City and quickly became the team's best player. On February 18, 1904, Forrest and his KCAC club did what was becoming an Allen brother rite of passage: they crushed Naismith's Kansas Jayhawks by a score of 27–10.

Phog became the area's biggest basketball talent and an astute promoter of the game. In a sold-out Kansas City arena, Allen led the KCAC Blue Diamonds to victory over the AAU champion Buffalo Germans. Naismith ended up officiating the deciding game and was very impressed with Allen. In what may have been his one and only brush with recruiting, Naismith approached Phog about bringing his talents to Lawrence the following year to suit up for the Jayhawks. Little did Naismith know at the time, Phog's previous trips to Lawrence to watch his brother Pete had already convinced him that KU would be his college destination.

On February 8, 1906, Phog played his first game for the Jayhawks in a 40–10 victory over the Wyandotte Athletic Club. The next day he was part of the KU squad that defeated the Independent Athletic Club 43–16. The Jayhawks finished the year with a record of 12–7, their most successful record to date. Allen's importance to the team had been lost on no one, including Naismith. In a team meeting in the PE director's office, the young Allen was unanimously voted by his teammates as captain for the following season.

Basketball's burgeoning popularity was traveling through the state of Kansas like wildfire and Phog was all too eager to fuel it at every chance. Baker University, a small liberal arts college and the oldest college in the state, also had a basketball program in its infantile stages. During his freshman season, Phog traveled the twenty miles to Baldwin City to help out the Baker squad, assisting the players with the game's basic fundamentals. At the time, the idea of actually coaching basketball was relatively nonexistent. Naismith himself spent the majority of his time busy with teaching classes and leading the chapel service on campus. He rarely traveled to road games, and the home games he did attend, he would often work as the referee.

Naismith did not see the need for someone to serve as basketball coach. So when Naismith received a letter from Baker officials as to whether Allen would like to officially coach the Baker squad for the upcoming season, Naismith called Allen into his office to discuss it.

"I've got a good joke for you, you bloody beggar," Naismith reportedly told Allen. "They want you to coach basketball down at Baker."

"What's so funny about that?" Allen said.

"Why, you can't coach basketball, you just play it," Naismith famously replied.

This last line would live on to be one of Naismith's most memorable quotes, accurately capturing the lack of importance Naismith placed on coaching basketball. While he didn't see the value of coaching, Naismith certainly saw the value of winning. He understood that winning improved the players' morale. Winning filled the stands and with the stands full, he had a much better chance of achieving his ultimate goal: to build a new gymnasium for basketball and gymnastics. Nobody had ever drawn a crowd like Phog, and his freshman year the rafters were filled to capacity. Losing his star player to Baker could prove devastating to Naismith's plans. But was Allen really willing to put an end to his college career to take on an unprecedented career choice and coach basketball at Baker University?

Phog's Baker offer included room and board as well as a stipend. The Allen family did not have the necessary means to provide a financial cushion for Phog during his time in college and in just one year his bills were piling up. So Allen did what he had to do to survive and left the University of Kansas after only one year to accept the position of head coach at Baker University

The following season, with Allen down the road cutting his coaching teeth, the Jayhawks huddled around their anti-coach, Naismith. The Phog-less squad returned to their losing ways finishing the year 7–8. This included a 39–24 dismantling at the hands of none other than Phog Allen's Baker team. The *University Daily Kansan* reported what was becoming clear to many. "Dr. James Naismith, the inventor of the game, is so busy with his work as athletic director that he rarely finds the time give the men through training."

After the 1907 season, Naismith decided to focus on his physical education department, and now the Jayhawks found themselves in a precarious situation: coach-less, with an athletic director in Naismith who struggled to see the significance of filling such a role. But the popularity of basketball was at an all time high, especially on the campuses of Midwest universities. To satiate this excitement, the Missouri Valley Athletic Conference was formed with five schools including Kansas, Missouri, Iowa, Nebraska, and Washington University in St. Louis. Kansas had done its part, readying the newly constructed Robinson Gymnasium for the intercollegiate competition that was on the verge of exploding. On December 13, 1907, the Kansas basketball team got the building off to a glowing start by destroying Ottawa 66–22. Kansas followed that game to an 18–6 record and the first Missouri Valley Conference championship going 6–0 in conference play. The next year the Jayhawks won their first 19 games, finishing 25–3 and winning their second Missouri Valley Conference championship in as many years. Sitting in the stands for home games, quietly watching from the same seat was the game's inventor, James Naismith. On the sideline, coaching for the Jayhawks was Naismith's first coaching hire, none other than Forrest Claire Allen. The legacy had begun.

The Journey

Monday, November 22: 18 Days Until Auction

I woke up and called Justin Unell at the urging of my father. I had never met Justin before. He was ten years younger than me, and I had left Kansas long before he'd grown up. But Justin was the son of my parents' friends, and was now working at the local NBC affiliate in Kansas City. I doubted as to whether he'd have any interest in helping me out considering we'd never met, but I needed to get the word out knowing I couldn't possibly rely on the few booster meetings I had set up. I thought, *Maybe there'd be some wealthy Kansas fan out there that'd love to be a part of this?*

I knew I needed to get in front of the media and figured where better to do it than in Kansas City? I gave Justin a call, and he was happy to help. He said he could put my story on the news desk and if a reporter found it compelling, perhaps they'd give me a call. I thanked him for his time and set my sights on my first alumnus meeting.

I was on my way to Lawrence to meet with Dana Anderson, who had donated funds to help build the Anderson Family Football Complex, which housed training facilities for the Kansas football program. Anderson was a 1959 KU grad from nearby Salina. He had risen to tremendous success as the vice-chairman of The Macerich Group, a company involved in the acquisition, development, and management of shopping centers located throughout the United States.

On the way up Highway K-10 to see Dana, a pit in the bottom of my stomach began to form. The thought of asking a complete stranger for a large sum of money had me feeling quite uneasy. I also felt guilty for putting him on the spot, knowing here was a man who'd done nothing but support the university he loved.

Anderson resided permanently in Santa Monica where his business was headquartered. He made frequent visits back to

Lawrence and this particular trip had him in town to spend Thanksgiving with his family. As we pulled into the driveway of his son's home, I gathered my thoughts and tried to remind myself that my cause was indeed a noble one. I walked up to the doorway as Avi and Daymion filmed behind me. I only imagined what this ridiculous scene looked like to neighbors in this quiet Lawrence suburb. I rang the doorbell. I waited. I rang again. I waited. I rang again. Finally it became clear that nobody was home.

When Dana answered his cell phone, it seemed clear that the quick conversation we had the week prior had been rather low on his scale of importance—so low that I had to remind him that the conversation actually took place. He quickly apologized and informed us he'd be back to the house immediately. So we sat and waited for him to arrive.

The minute he stepped out of his car, much of my anxiety began to dissipate. Dana's smile and firm handshake seemed to confirm that his Kansas traits had not been wiped away by his years spent in California. We located a couple chairs inside the house and began the interview. I started by asking Dana about his connection to KU.

"Well, I am just a huge fan," he said. "I've been fortunate enough in my life to be economically successful. And they've been the primary beneficiary of my charitable giving."

From there we spoke about the basketball program and Dana recalled some of his favorite moments. We spoke about the rules and the upcoming auction in a general sense. As he spoke, I nodded as if I was listening closely, but I wasn't. I was worried about the last question I had to ask. I felt like Michael Corleone with the gun in my hand, pretending to listen to Sollozzo but waiting to pull the trigger. Finally, I couldn't put it off any longer.

"Dana, the last thing I want to do is put you on the spot. Um, that's not my intention at all. But um, you know, um, we have twenty days until the auction. And what um, what I'm trying to do is put a team together to bid and win this auction. Um, what are your thoughts on that?"

Dana paused. The jig was up. "Um," he said, unsure of how to respond. "Well I think it would be a great addition to the university and to the Hall of Fame, I just don't think the economics are feasible. And, while I think they belong there—fully appropriate they be there—I am committed in making significant contributions every year under my current budget so, I have a pretty full plate."

I knew Dana had given a tremendous amount of money to build the Anderson Family Football Complex, but it turns out that he was still paying for other capital improvements around campus as well. He had pledged a yearly commitment to the university that far exceeded anything I or anyone else could begin to comprehend.

Even though the interview hadn't gone as I'd hoped, I was relieved that it was over. We said our goodbyes and he wished me luck. A true gentleman, if Dana had any hard feelings about our meeting, he sure did a good job of hiding it. As we started on our way back to Overland Park, my phone rang. A woman on the other end said, "This is Amy Hawley from NBC News in Kansas City. I found your story on the news desk. I have a feeling our viewers would like this," she said. "We're going to put you on the news. Can you be here in thirty minutes?" Daymion hit the pedal and we raced back down K-10 and out of Lawrence towards Kansas City.

Tuesday, November 23: 17 Days Until Auction

My first television appearance aired the night before on the local NBC affiliate. It felt like I finally had a little momentum and I could sense some local buzz developing. This was confirmed when I received a call in the morning from a gentleman named Todd Leabo. He explained that he was a producer for the radio show *Between the Lines*, hosted by Kevin Kietzman on 810 AM Radio. NBC news anchor Amy Hawley had told him about what I was trying to do and he wanted to know if I'd like to call in to the show that day. I was thrilled because I knew that in Kansas City (and most metropolitan areas), radio is often a far more effective way to reach sports fans than television. I was also thrilled because *Between the Lines* was the most popular radio show in town, but I did have a bit of doubt about host Kevin Kietzman. Kietzman was a Kansas State grad and had come under fire from some Jayhawk fans for being anti-KU at times. For this reason, I had some question as to why he'd want to feature a KU fan like myself, especially one on a wild goose chase.

But it turns out my paranoia radar had been raised by reading one too many misguided message board posts. Kietzman ended up having me on the air for a whopping fifteen minutes, plugging my website several times and urging listeners to reach out and contact me. "I think Allen Fieldhouse would be a great place for those rules," he even said as we wrapped up the interview. When it was over with, I wondered how many people had heard it.

Many, as it would turn out.

Emails began rolling in, with KU fans pledging everything from $10 to $20 to $100. Before I could even make sense of it all, Daymion, Avi, and I said goodbye to Grammy and headed to the airport to jump on a plane for Phoenix. We were off to see another prominent KU booster.

Wednesday, November 24: 16 Days Until Auction

I woke up in Phoenix to find emails from even more KU fans that had reached out, pledging their help because they had seen me on TV and heard me on the radio. Though I felt grateful to be a part of "the best fans in college basketball," I decided that I couldn't start taking small donations from people. Even if they added up to a substantial amount, it wouldn't be close to enough, and then I'd be left in the difficult position of returning money to everyone.

Now someone pledging hundreds of thousands of dollars would of course be a different story. So I perused the hundreds of emails hoping one such message would stand out from the rest. And sure enough, one did. This email didn't pledge any money. This email only pledged help. This email read:

> *I heard the end of Josh's interview on 810 Sports today. How can we help? My husband, Dr. Mark Allen, is Phog Allen's grandson.* —Louise Allen

Louise Allen was the wife of Dr. Mark Allen, the son of Bob Allen, who had played for his father, Phog Allen at KU. I couldn't believe that the ancestors of Phog Allen had reached out to me. The Allen name was still revered in Kansas and getting them on my side had the potential to be a game changer. I quickly emailed Louise back and we set up a phone call for the following morning. In the meantime, I had more pressing matters requiring my undivided attention.

Today would be a big day as I was meeting with Stewart Horesji, the second prominent KU booster I had made arrangements to interview. A 1959 graduate of KU, Horesji had great success as a businessman, entrepreneur, and investor. He began by running his family's welding supply firm in Salina, Kansas, and used profits from the business to invest in Berkshire Hathaway, a firm controlled by celebrity investor Warren Buffett. In 1999, Stewart finished construction on the Horesji Family Athletics Center, which sat directly behind Allen Fieldhouse and housed volleyball courts while doubling as a basketball practice facility.

As we began our climb high into the hills of Phoenix where Horesji lived, the feeling of unease returned. I decided there was simply no way around this feeling; I'd just have to deal with it to the best of my abilities. Besides, the simple fact was that I couldn't tell these boosters I was coming to ask for money, or they never would have agreed to see me. If at the end of my plea they decided not to get involved, well, that was totally and completely their prerogative and I would not make any judgments whatsoever. On top of that, if they instructed me after the interview that they would not like me to use the footage, then I would delete it forever. (They would have to sign a release after the interview giving us permission to use it.) I was simply there to make a friendly case for capitalizing on a moment in history that I felt would never come again.

Upon Stewart answering the door of his home, my anxiety once again melted away. Stewart had as friendly and calming a manner as I'd ever encountered. Like Dana Anderson before him, I was starting to think there was something to humility and success. Both men, while highly decorated in the business world, had managed to hold onto the common trait that had long defined residents from my home state: kindness.

A quick tour of Stewart's home showed off an assortment of special Jayhawk memorabilia he'd received throughout the years. Unique artifacts and gifts from athletic directors and coaches lined his office shelves. In another room, an old Allen Fieldhouse Jayhawk decal was signed over by then coach Roy Williams, thanking Stewart for his contributions to pay for some much needed locker room renovations.

Stewart and I finally settled into his living room to begin our formal interview. I decided that with him, for his curiosity and my health alike, I would get into the reason behind my visit quickly. I figured there was no sense in stringing along Stewart or my pounding heart.

After asking him about his connection to KU and Kansas basketball, I jumped right into the rules. Stewart was already aware of the auction but had not really considered it in depth. "Where do you think the rules should be?" I asked him.

"Well, that's a good question," he replied. "I suppose it would be nice to have it in the museum on campus."

I wanted to hammer the point home more. "As you probably know, Dr. Naismith spent forty-one years of his life in Lawrence. He's buried there. We play on Naismith Drive on James Naismith Court across from Naismith Hall . . . seems to me that the best place would be that hall of athletics right there."

"I agree with you," said Stewart. "That would be perfect."

"I'm going around the country trying to raise money to go to this auction on December 10 and win these rules," I said. "I'm not here to put you on the spot, Stewart. I come in the friend-liest way possible, but I'm out here asking for your help?"

"Uh huh," Stewart said as if the reason behind my visit had finally come into complete focus for him. "You said the auction is December 10?"

"Yes it is," I replied.

"Well I'd give it some consideration," Stewart said. "I'd have to discuss it with my wife, but I do think she's more in favor of doing things for little kids than tradition."

I of course would never want to get in the way of his other charitable efforts and told him as much. As pleasant and warm as Stewart was, I knew almost immediately that he wouldn't be able to help. Though it was clear his love for Kansas ran deep, I could tell this was not something he viewed as paramount. We shared a polite goodbye and I set off on my way.

As Daymion guided the rental car down the long and windy road toward the greater Phoenix area, doubt began to creep into my mind. For the first time, I wondered whether I was chasing an impossible pipe dream. Until this point, I had figured that my enthusiasm would be enough to get others excited, but Dana hadn't gotten very excited. Stewart hadn't gotten very excited either. While I was doing a decent job of presenting the facts of the upcoming auction, I wasn't connecting with these men on a personal level. There was no sense of camaraderie; there existed no feeling of two Kansas boys from different genera-tions connecting on the one thing Kansas boys had connected on for 100 plus years: Jayhawk basketball. I was failing to stir up that swelling pride in the basketball tradition at KU that I was certain lived in them, just like it did in me. I had failed to convince them how the rules coming to KU would forever cement our basketball legacy. I had left them unconvinced that urgent action was necessary.

As we settled into the long drive to Las Vegas, something suddenly occurred to me, something so obvious I was upset that I hadn't thought of it sooner: my voice wasn't enough. I was just one person, a random fan off the street. If I was going to convince anyone, then maybe I needed more fans to back me up. And perhaps, I needed to let some other more recognizable people do the talking.

In preparation for my final scheduled meeting with David Booth, I decided I would make a video featuring fans, players, personalities, and anyone else who would support the purpose of my mission. I was hoping this video would serve as the ultimate testimony to help me convince David Booth how important this was.

After arriving at our Las Vegas hotel, we were greeted by my brother, Micah, who had driven from California to catch the Jayhawks play in the Las Vegas Invitational. Like Micah, our arrival in Vegas had been planned, but my final pitch with David Booth was largely coincidental. Booth just happened to be arriving in Las Vegas for an executive conference two days after the tournament's conclusion. In the meantime, I was hopeful I could get in front of fans and alumni to testify on camera for the video I wanted to play for David Booth.

7

THE DISCIPLES

THE UNIVERSITY OF Kansas hired James Naismith for his grasp of traditional religion, not basketball, the new one he had created. A young man named Phog Allen soon made his way to Lawrence to learn the fundamentals of this new game from the creator himself. The two men were very close. But on the subject of basketball they were worlds apart. For James Naismith, basketball was absolutely not his personal manifestation for world domination. Naismith saw basketball as nothing more than a recreational pastime for the cold winter months. When the weather turned warm again, Naismith would just assume the kids be playing outside.

Allen, on the other hand, saw a young game with unlimited potential. To the fiery young coach, this was a game akin to football, one which young men could fiercely compete to win in. Allen suspected that basketball could also be a tool to turn boys into men, and Allen's hunch was that to do so required a coach who could be a passionate and enthusiastic leader. So when

Phog Allen stood on the sideline at the University of Kansas at the dawn of the Roaring Twenties, it was he, not Naismith, who became the game's most visible figurehead. And it was Allen who would inspire a new generation of young men to pursue the basketball coaching profession.

Allen's first two coaching disciples were KU players John Lonborg and John Bunn, both who graduated in 1920. Lonborg went on to coach for twenty-three years and guide Northwestern University to the 1931 Helms National Championship. Bunn would head to Stanford where he built the Cardinal program into a national power, winning the 1937 Helms Title and putting West Coast basketball on the map.

Allen's next great protégé would be a local boy from Halstead, Kansas, named Adolph Rupp. From 1919 to 1923, Rupp mostly watched as Paul Endacott led KU to back-to-back Helms National Titles in 1922 and 1923. Rupp played sparingly over the course of his career, but from the shadows he closely studied the masterful Allen and picked the brain of Naismith whenever he had the chance. By Rupp's senior year, it was common knowledge that he wanted to be a coach, and Allen was not only supportive, but even let Rupp call plays. In this respect, Adolph Rupp may have been the first person ever groomed to be a head basketball coach while still in college.

Upon his graduation from KU, Rupp coached high school basketball, first in Kansas, and then in Illinois. Then Rupp got the chance of a lifetime. The head coach from the University of Illinois—a man named Craig Ruby—recommended Rupp to the University of Kentucky when their coaching job became available in 1929. While it's inconceivable to imagine a high school coach getting such a job today, at that time, such a move was considered to be more the normal course of business. So just six years after graduating from Kansas, Adolph Rupp was hired as the head basketball coach at the University of Kentucky, a position he would keep for the next forty-two years.

Wasting little time, Rupp immediately built Kentucky into a perennial powerhouse. "The Baron of the Bluegrass," as Rupp would later be known, would go on to lead Kentucky to four National Championships, winning twenty-seven conference titles and 876 games in the process. In the Bluegrass State, Kentucky basketball quickly became a way of life, passionately subscribed to by a devout fan base. Post-Rupp, Kentucky has sustained tremendous success and now claims eight National Championships and more wins than any other program in history (including ten more games than the University of Kansas, who sits second on the list). Thanks to Rupp, Kentucky basketball became the first major offshoot from KU and Rupp became the next disciple to fall off the Allen coaching tree.

If the 1920s for Phog were about winning basketball games and promoting his profession, the 1930s were about cementing the game next to the giants of the time: baseball and football. Basketball's biggest issue was its lack of unity and organization. Most frustrating to Allen and Naismith were the rules changes that were spinning out of control on a yearly basis. To deal with a segmented game—one that lacked a central unifying committee—Allen called a summit of fellow coaches. They showed up for the first meeting of what would become the National Association of Basketball Coaches. Phog, the group's initial organizer, was elected president. At Phog's suggestion, the NABC named Naismith its honorary chairman.

Phog turned his attention to what he felt was a glaring void in the landscape of college basketball: there was no unanimous national champion. At the following NABC meeting, Allen proposed such a national, season-ending tournament and launched a committee to work with the NCAA on the initiative. In 1939, the inaugural NCAA tournament took place, with Oregon defeating Ohio State for the title. In 1940, Kansas marched all the way to the national title game where they lost to the Indiana Hoosiers, 80–63.

The 1942 NCAA Tournament was indicative of just how important Allen had become in the landscape of basketball. KU would face Colorado and their head coach Frosty Cox. Forrest "Frosty" Cox had starred at Kansas from 1929 to 1931. His association with Allen got him the head-coaching job at Colorado University, where he stayed from 1936 to 1950.

Cox and Colorado squeezed by Allen and KU 46–44 before losing to eventual champion Stanford (coached by Allen protégé John Bunn). The loss meant the end of a stellar career for KU's star guard Ralph Miller. But Miller had also been influenced by Allen and went on to a remarkable coaching career of his own, coaching at Wichita State, Iowa, and Oregon State, compiling a 657–382 overall record in thirty-eight seasons.

Kansas had become the foremost basketball finishing school in the country, which is exactly why a young African American man named John McClendon had arrived at KU some years prior. McClendon showed up in Lawrence before inter-collegiate athletics were integrated, so he was unable to suit up for the Jayhawks. But still he would leave Kansas to become one of the foremost pioneers in American sports history, winning three consecutive NAIA championships at Tennessee State, and eventually becoming the first African American head coach in professional sports.

McClendon, Rupp, Bunn, Lonborg, Cox, and Miller all had attended the University of Kansas and would all eventually land in the Basketball Hall of Fame. When a local Kansas boy named Dean Smith enrolled at KU in the fall of 1949, he hoped he might pick up some of the same insight the others had.

In 1952, Dean's junior year, the Jayhawks were a national power behind star center Clyde Lovellette out of Indiana. Allen had beaten out Indiana and Kentucky in a heated recruiting battle and Lovellette had proved to be well worth it, leading Kansas all the way to the NCAA title game against St. John's, the rising New York City program coached by Frank McGuire.

For Allen so much was riding on the title game. The year of 1952 was an Olympic cycle, which meant the National Champions would send a team and coaching staff to the trials in New York City for a chance to represent the country at the Helsinki Olympics. On top of that, when the NCAA Tournament began, with the regularity that KU was winning, it seemed a foregone conclusion that KU would eventually break through. But thirteen years had passed since Allen and his NABC cohorts had founded the NCAA Tournament and Phog had yet to win it. Allen, now at sixty-six years old, was well aware of a state law mandating all public employees retire at age seventy. In the twilight of his career, he had to wonder if he'd ever have this chance again.

Fittingly, Phog Allen and the Jayhawks wiped the floor with the Johnnies. Behind Clyde Lovellette's 33 points KU won going away 80–63. Even Dean Smith got on the floor for the last 29 seconds of the title game. Three days after winning the

NCAA title the Jayhawks opened the Olympic trials by meeting the NIT champ LaSalle at Madison Square Garden. The winner of the game would provide half the Olympic team roster and one coach. Behind 40 points from Lovellette, KU pulled out a gutsy win despite being down 13 points in the second half. The Jayhawks were headed to Helsinki. In Helsinki, the KU squad along with the AAU champion Peoria Caterpillar Diesels marched all the way to the gold medal, defeating the Russians 36–25 in the final.

After graduation, Dean Smith served as assistant coach under Phog Allen for one season, before heading into a bigger assistant's role at Air Force. From there Smith would go on to be lead assistant under Frank McGuire at North Carolina, the same Frank McGuire who KU had beaten in the '52 final. After the 1961 season Dean Smith would replace McGuire as head coach of the Tar Heels, a position he would keep until 1997.

Over the course of thirty-six years, Smith would build North Carolina into a powerhouse program, winning two national titles and appearing in eleven Final Fours. After Adolph Rupp, Dean Smith would launch the next basketball religion to stem from Kansas—this one not Kansas Blue . . . or Kentucky Blue, but its own shade of Carolina Blue. Three of the most iconic basketball buildings on the planet, Rupp Arena in Lexington, Kentucky, the Dean Dome in Chapel Hill, North Carolina, and Allen Fieldhouse in Lawrence, Kansas, are named after coaching legends who were first Jayhawks.

James Naismith was not a man who stubbornly held onto principle when he was proved to be wrong—and on the subject of coaching Naismith had been dead wrong. Proof lied not just in Allen's accomplishments but in all of the coaching disciples to stem from KU and forge their own legendary careers. Late in his life Naismith signed a sketched picture of himself over to Phog Allen that seemed to serve as the ultimate act of contrition. It said, "from the father of basketball to the father of basketball coaching."

But long before he signed that poster over shortly before his death, Allen had proved Naismith wrong in another, more important way. Allen had proved beyond a shadow of doubt that basketball was not simply a game intended for recreational purposes. Allen had turned basketball into what he always suspected it could be, a mighty peer of football and baseball.

When Allen retired in 1956, he had won 771 games, making him then, far and away, the winningest coach in the history of college basketball. He had won twenty-six conference championships, including an NCAA Championship and an Olympic Gold Medal. He had revolutionized the sport, a tireless promoter at every turn.

In a final dose of magic, Allen gave Kansas fans not one but two parting gifts. First, he persuaded the state legislature to spend an inordinate amount of money on a new fieldhouse for basketball at KU, and he then proceeded to oversee every last aspect of its construction. Next, he signed the greatest basketball player on the planet when he secured the services of the 7 foot 1 prep star Wilton Norman Chamberlain from Philadelphia, Pennsylvania. Considering what Allen Fieldhouse and Wilt Chamberlain would become, perhaps no coach in sports history has ever left a program in better shape than Phog Allen.

In September of 1972, Phog Allen died at the age of eighty-eight. "Doc will go down as the greatest basketball coach of all time. What I did was just an extension of what I learned from him," Adolph Rupp told the *Topeka Capitol* after his funeral.

The year prior to Allen's retirement, when Kansas officials were trying to figure out what name to give what would be a revolutionary new basketball arena, they were faced with a considerable dilemma. At the time there was an institutional policy that prevented on-campus buildings from bearing the name of a living person. Thus it appeared that naming the new arena after Phog Allen was not a possibility. It seemed logical that basketball's inventor, James Naismith, who had passed away over fifteen years prior, whose grave stood a mere mile from the new fieldhouse, would be a shoo-in for such an honor, and rightfully so. But as the arena neared completion, Allen supporters came flying out of the woodwork. Fellow and rival coaches, governors, senators and media members called upon the university to make an exception to the rule and honor a man who had done so much for the game, and for the young men he coached. The onslaught of support from every direction served as the ultimate recognition for the life's work of one man. In the final moments of construction, the regents held a secret meeting and decided to ignore the old rule and name the building after Phog.

For nearly six decades a gymnasium has sat on the campus of the University of Kansas, located on a street called Naismith Drive. Roughly twenty times per year, people make pilgrimages from all over to experience an inimitable religious gathering in this vaunted house of worship. In 2005, on the structure's fiftieth birthday, the *New York Times* ran a headline that read, "Kansas

Cathedral Turns 50." Some fifty years prior in 1955, KU's student newspaper ran a poll asking residents who they felt the arena should be named after. The results were resounding. Phog Allen received 92 percent of the votes, beating out James Naismith, the sport's creator, by a landslide. Looking down from the heavens, Phog's mother Mary must have been so proud.

The Journey

Saturday, November 27: 13 Days Until Auction

I finally was able to jump on the phone with Louise Allen and her husband, Dr. Mark Allen. Louise explained that she had caught the last twenty seconds of my radio interview and felt compelled to email me. When she introduced her husband who was also on the line, I was pretty sure the conversation would go nowhere. Louise was nice enough but Mark seemed rather annoyed. I got the sense his wife had dragged him onto the phone and that he had many other things he'd rather be doing on this Saturday morning.

Mark voiced his doubts about the rules making sense for Kansas. He shared with me some of KU's more pressing capital improvement initiatives and felt that given the athletic department's precarious situation in the wake of the ticket scandal, a fan-driven attempt to procure the rules was potentially a giant waste of time. Lastly, Mark wondered if Springfield wasn't a more appropriate resting place for the rules.

First, I explained the Hall of Fame's failed past and their inability to properly display the rules when they had them in their possession for nearly thirty years. I explained to Mark that the school's weakened position was actually more of a reason for us to get involved. If it wouldn't be the fans, then who would it be? The more I made a case, the more I felt Mark coming around. By the end of the call, the Allens had agreed to sit down with me when I was to be in Kansas City in a few days time.

I set off for the Orleans Arena to watch Kansas play in the finals of the Las Vegas Invitational. The Jayhawks had beaten Ohio the prior evening and were now set to battle the Arizona Wildcats for the championship. I arrived early so I could speak at a pep rally and collect more fan support for my video presentation.

Afterwards, I caught a glimpse of ESPN college basketball analyst Jay Bilas roaming the sideline in civilian clothes. Bilas played at Duke University in the early '80s, and had since emerged as one of the most well thought of and respected analysts in the game. I considered the video I was planning to play for David Booth. Aside from Seth Davis, most everyone I had filmed had supported me because, like me, they were Jayhawk fans. I needed someone neutral, and I decided that Bilas represented the ideal candidate.

I approached the former Duke player turned commentator to see if he might agree to an interview and where he thought the rules should end up. Bilas agreed to speak with me on the spot. He was well aware of the upcoming auction, and when it came to their appropriate destination, he failed to mince words.

"Well, I tend to think that Allen Fieldhouse is one of the two or three most important sports venues in the United States—in any sport, not just basketball. You walk in there and you can feel it. You feel the history of it. Heck, maybe all the KU alums better pick up a collection and have some proxy there to put in a bid so they have them. I mean, that's the right place for it. The good news is they know who invented the game and they know who wrote the first rules and there are copies of them everywhere. So that's not an issue, but having the originals would be awfully nice too. It's sort of like, where does the Declaration of Independence belong? It belongs in Washington DC at the National Archives and I think if it were my choice, I'd put them at KU, but people don't tend to listen to me." With that said, I was hoping that David Booth *would* listen.

We finally settled into our seats and watched the Jayhawks take on Arizona. As I stood next to Micah, Daymion, and Avi, I lost myself completely in the game. For the first time since I had left on this journey, I forgot about the rules and the stresses associated with raising money.

The game was close until the last few minutes at which point KU began to pull away. As the clock winded down, I surveyed the crowd around me. Here we were, one measly state away from Arizona, a short drive as far as alumni weekends in Vegas are considered—and the Orleans Arena, a college-sized gymnasium, half-a-mile off the Strip, was at least 70 percent full of Jayhawk fans. As we launched into the Rock Chalk Jayhawk chant, signifying yet another victory, I was reminded of the task at hand. It was these people I was doing this for. These people that Seth Davis had called, "the greatest college basketball fans in the nation." These hoop fanatics who would follow their team to Vegas, Hawaii, or Russia for that matter. I decided that I couldn't let them down. I would go as hard as I could until the very last moment.

The win capped off what had been a perfect day. My brother Micah and I had shared so many amazing Kansas basketball experiences: Final Fours, National Championships, and victorious road trips to a multitude of college towns. But this was different. This day had been unique. It had started with the first family of Kansas basketball—the Allens, who were now willing to meet with me in person. It had continued with an unexpected and convincing Jay Bilas interview, and had ended with a resounding Jayhawk victory.

With the Booth meeting only a couple days away and the hard work to pick up the following morning, we knew this would be our last night to enjoy Vegas like Vegas was meant to be enjoyed. Micah had an idea for us to find a tattoo parlor and get our skin inscribed with our love for Kansas basketball.

I had never harbored any grand plans to cover my body in permanent ink, but I was intrigued by Micah's idea. If I was going to pull off something extraordinary, it seemed like I needed to step out of my comfort zone. On top of the good luck it might bring, if Micah were willing to go through with it as well, then I couldn't possibly back down. And so it was an unspoken game of "chicken" on this night that carried us into the tattoo parlor around the corner from the Orleans Arena.

As we contemplated designs and placement and size, I considered Judaism's hard stance on tattoos. The Torah states quite explicitly: "You shall not make gashes in your flesh . . . or incise any marks on yourselves." I considered the old wives' tale that individuals with tattoos were not allowed to be buried inside Jewish cemeteries.

With more pressing matters at hand than my burial location, I watched as Micah sat down with the tattoo artist first. He had arrived at a symbolic design to prominently display his faith to anyone who ever saw him shirtless. On his heart, Micah decided on placing an outline of the state of Kansas. A basketball would then be drawn inside state lines as to mark the exact location of the city of Lawrence. Then it was my turn. I had decided on a basketball with the word "Kansas" written on it, which was placed on my upper arm just below my right shoulder. As we walked out of the tattoo parlor with our newly minted tattoos, one thing was certain: What had happened in Vegas certainly wasn't going to stay there.

Tuesday, November 30: 10 Days Until Auction

The day had finally arrived. Micah had returned to California on Sunday and we were back to the original three of Daymion, Avi, and myself. I had spent the last two days working hard to edit the Booth video in a way that would play both quickly and effectively. We had decided to make the meeting as convenient as possible for Booth, so we rented a room at the Aria Hotel and Casino where he was staying. As I picked up my room key, I considered the metaphorical reality of my plight. I was going to be on the twenty-first floor of a Las Vegas hotel room, and I was going all in, hoping to hit blackjack.

After testing the video and setting up the cameras, we sat and waited for Booth to arrive. When he didn't show up the minute he was supposed to, a wave of fear washed over me. In all of my preparations, I had failed to check back in with Deborah Foster, his assistant, to confirm our meeting. Booth had been in Fiji, having just returned to the States two days prior, and I feared that Deborah had perhaps failed to remind him of our scheduled meeting. And if she had, I feared that something more important had come up. As I cracked the door of our hotel room in an attempt to make it more inviting, I wondered if someone like David Booth would ever simply walk into a random hotel room? But sure enough, shortly after the door opened and a "hello" was muttered, I shot out of my seat to greet him.

"Hello," I said as kindly and as energetic as possible, hoping to make it clear he was walking into a safe place.

"David Booth," he responded as he held out his hand.

"I'm Josh Swade," I said as I grabbed his hand and looked him in the eye.

He cut right to the chase. "What's this all about, might I ask?"

"Of course. Well, we are doing a documentary on Kansas basketball."

"Oh, okay?" Booth said as if to suggest he needed a little more info.

"I live in New York City and I came across the news that James Naismith's original rules of basketball would be coming up for auction at Sotheby's," I replied.

"I actually grew up on Naismith Drive," he said.

"I know," I responded. "That's a big reason why you're here."

With that, Booth chuckled and took a seat. He seemed at the very least to be amused enough to see what this was all about. Before I even had the chance to ask him a question, he began to talk about his connection to Kansas basketball.

"You know, whenever I go back, that last twelve minutes before the game starts, all of these memories from my childhood come crashing back. I think of coming to games with my parents. It almost brings a tear to my eye."

I immediately felt a connection to David. His feelings about Kansas basketball mirrored my own. For him, it was a constant reminder to the simpler times of his youth.

"What was it like growing up at 1931 Naismith Drive, literally down the street from the doors to the shrine we call Allen Fieldhouse?" I asked him.

"It was spectacular," he said. "We would often go sneak up into one of the side doors and I can remember a shoot around before practice started with players like Dee Ketchum and Jerry Garner. They would let us talk and come in and shoot baskets with them."

Booth continued to wax poetic about his childhood and his experience as a student at KU. As I listened to him speak I found myself so enthralled that I would momentarily forget about why I was there in the first place. But the cameras pointed in our faces were reminder enough, returning me to reality time and again. Finally I couldn't put it off anymore. It was time to explain to him what this was all about. First I had a video to play him.

"David, I went to Sotheby's about three weeks ago to see James Naismith's original rules of basketball, which as you know, are coming up for auction in ten days time. That was such a profound experience that it's led me across the country to meet with all kinds of people, including yourself, and so I'd like to show you a little clip of what we've done. Can I show you?"

"Oh absolutely."

Avi hit play on the DVD player and images began flying off the screen, from Cole Aldrich to Drew Gooden to Jay Bilas to fan after fan after fan. As the video built to its emotional peak, I snuck a glance in Booth's direction in an attempt to gauge his interest in the video. I feared he would find this all trivial, nothing more than amusing—or even worse—a complete and utter waste of time.

But my glance in his direction put all my fears to rest. Booth was watching the screen with extreme focus, a skill he had likely depended on time and again in the business world. Hanging on each word of every testimony, it was clear that he was into it. When the video was finished, I got right to it.

"David, the last thing I am trying to do is put you on the spot. That's not my intention at all. What you've already done for the university and the athletic department goes so far beyond anything I could ever comprehend. But what brings me here tonight are these rules. This is a chance in history. We will never get this chance again. Someone is going to get this document. And it belongs in our shrine."

"You're right, it belongs there," he replied.

"So how do we get this done?" I asked.

Booth thought to himself for a moment.

"Well, I would be very happy to be a lead sponsor in this project. I'll do more than my fair share to get this thing done."

"That's amazing," I replied. As excited as I was to hear that he wanted in, there wasn't enough time to beat around the bush. I needed to know what he was thinking money-wise.

"Based on what I've heard, I think to have a shot, we need to be in the $3 million range."

Booth thought to himself for another moment. "Well, I'll be happy to do at least a third of it. But, I'd like to see some other participation. At three million, I'd love to have other participants."

"Absolutely," I said. "A million puts us in the game. We have to at least be in the hunt."

"Yes, we've got to be in the hunt," he responded.

"They can't end up at another university," I added.

"No, that would be devastating," he agreed.

"So, I guess we've got a plan here," I said.

"Well I suppose we do," said Booth. "It still seems like a long shot, but it's still a better shot than you had yesterday. As you talk to other people, tell them I'm good for a million. Unfortunately, the number of people you can call on the list is fairly short. But if we can get three or four people together, then we might have a shot."

Wednesday, December 1: 9 Days Until Auction

After the previous night's meeting and the million-dollar commitment from Booth, I landed at the Kansas City airport feeling hopeful. I raced to the local Fox TV affiliate for an interview, as the sports news anchor had reached out when he caught wind of my push to bring the rules to KU. I agreed to the interview for two reasons: I still had to get back to Kansas to meet with the Allens, and I was in no position to turn down any overture from the media, especially considering my race against the clock. Though I had completed my meetings with the "Big 3," I felt as though an unidentified, deep-pocketed KU alum could still step forward if he or she caught wind of my mission.

Despite a lack of sleep, I managed to do a decent enough job during the interview. They told me it would air on that evening's news, and I hoped it would come across the television screen of a difference maker I could add to the Booth commitment. After all, it was the radio interview that had gotten me to the Allens. Now it was time to hustle over to their house to see if I could get them on my side.

On the way over to the Allens' home, my phone rang. I recognized the Austin, Texas, area code. I hoped the voice on the other end would be David Booth, but instead I immediately recognized the unmistakable Australian accent of his assistant,

Deborah Foster. I feared for a moment that Deborah would be upset with me. With her, I had arranged the Booth meeting in Vegas, but in our series of conversations, I had failed to be completely forthcoming. Now that David had likely shared the details of our meeting, I thought she would scold me for hitting her boss up for money. I readied my most sincere apology, an apology that was nothing less than the truth. I would tell her that I couldn't have possibly revealed my true intentions, as she never would have allowed me such access. It had simply been a means to an end.

But Deborah's firm grasp of the big picture became immediately evident the minute she opened her mouth. It was at this moment that I fully understood just what type of person I was dealing with in Deborah Foster. How silly of me to think she would be offended by the minutia of my approach. That was history now. Deborah Foster understood that this was business, and not personal.

She quickly informed me that David had indeed filled her in on the details of our meeting. We discussed the auction for a moment and the logistics of David bidding. While I pushed to cement these details, Deborah interrupted me and said there had been a new development. Her tone suggested what she was about to tell me was not good news.

Deborah proceeded to read me the details of a message from an individual within the Kansas Athletic Department. The message stated that KU had heard of David's interest in bidding on the rules, but that they had some information to share with him. She said that KU had subsequently told David that the rules might not be real . . . as in might not be authentic . . . as in might be fake. As such, Deborah ultimately revealed that David was of course having second thoughts.

I was stunned by the news, and unsure of how to respond. I of course wasn't experienced or informed enough to comment on the legitimacy of the rules in any shape or manner whatsoever. I hung up with Deborah, stupefied. Here I was, pushing a boulder up a mountain . . . and for what? To win some kind of forged document?

I always knew that the likelihood of the school trying to derail my efforts was high once they caught wind of my actions. I knew that what I was doing would be frowned upon by the university. I understood that athletic departments have their own agendas, their own bureaucracy, and a laundry list of financial needs. I fully understood that the last thing KU needed was some fan out on the road trying to solicit their biggest donors for reasons not endorsed by them.

I knew all of that, but I carried on anyway. Because as I saw it, this was bigger than them. This was bigger than me. This was bigger than people in positions that wouldn't be in those positions in thirty years. Personnel at universities rotate like revolving doors. Players, coaches, even fans come and go. But this was something that would live on long after we had all left this earth.

But the university's suggestion that the rules might be inauthentic left me speechless. How could an auction house as reputable as Sotheby's ever bring to auction something other than the authentic rules of basketball? One thing I knew for certain; I wanted nothing to do with anything other than the original rules of basketball, the same ones that hung in the gymnasium that day in 1891 when Naismith introduced the game at the Springfield YMCA.

I hung up the phone with Deborah, unsure of what to do next. I wondered if I should just let this dream die. Should I just go back to New York, back to my family, back to my job, back to my old life? Why did KU doubt the rules' authenticity? Was this just a strategic ploy to scare alums away or was there real evidence? I couldn't call the school. I knew they'd never come clean with me. But I knew someone who could help. So I immediately headed over to the home of Mark and Louise Allen. If they felt compelled to assist me, then surely they could speed dial any number of connected individuals tied into privileged university affairs.

Upon settling into the Allen basement, it finally hit me where I was. Covering the room was an assortment of the most amazing memorabilia a Kansas basketball fan could ever hope to see. I scanned the room and saw everything, from Phog's letterman sweater, to a miniature statue of Phog, to old basketball photos and artwork. But it was something else that caught my eye. There, framed on the wall, was a copy of the rules of basketball themselves. This copy of the rules, said Mark, "had been given to Phog by Naismith."

As Mark and I studied them closely, I dove right into the issue at hand. I explained everything that had happened to that point in time: how I read about the auction and felt compelled to do something; how I left my job and family in New York to meet with alumni; how the night before David Booth had pledged a million dollars to the cause. I finished with the recent issue of the rules' authenticity. With time running out, I asked Mark and Louise point blank to help me.

I could sense that Louise was totally on board. It was Mark who was reluctant to get involved. As a busy physician Mark certainly didn't have the time to be bothered. On top of that I was a complete stranger off the street.

But my message to Mark was clear: "never again would this opportunity present itself." After parking myself on a couch in the Allen basement and giving them no indication that I would actually leave their home, I felt Mark begin to turn. He shared with me a story of particular note. He explained how he and his family had years prior set out to have a statue of Phog erected in front of Allen Fieldhouse. The Kansas athletic administration at the time had been against the statue and would not support the fundraising efforts necessary to afford such an undertaking. Undeterred, the Allen family took the matter into their own hands and raised the money themselves. After the statue was completed they told the administration, "you better get ready because we're showing up with the statue whether you like it or not."

The Allen family prevailed over the administrators in charge at the time. Today the Phog Allen statue stands as an iconic part of the Allen Fieldhouse experience. It has and will continue to be enjoyed by generations to come. To think it almost didn't happen because of employees in temporary positions hit right to the heart of my argument.

Mark understood that this was bigger than any one administration. He also seemed to grasp the ticking clock we were up against. We both were certain of one thing. We had to figure out the authenticity riddle. Mark professed his willingness to help. Excited to have him on board, I booked a plane ticket for the next morning back to New York to meet with the auction experts in person.

8

THE DESTRUCTION

DICK HARP HAD played for Phog Allen at KU from 1938 to 1940. After being a captain on the 1940 squad that lost in the National Championship, Harp went on to William Jewell College in Missouri where he served as a head coach for two years. Harp left William Jewell to join Allen's KU staff in 1948 and had been a KU assistant for eight seasons. So when Phog Allen was forced into retirement at the state-mandated age of seventy, it was Dick Harp who was chosen as his replacement.

Succeeding the greatest coach the game had ever seen, there would be no grace period for Harp in year one. With the greatest player in the country, Wilt Chamberlain, on his team, everyone expected Kansas to march straight to a national title. Anything less would be a monumental disappointment.

When the season began it appeared the Jayhawks would in fact live up to the hype as they pummeled the competition en route to a 12–0 start and a number one ranking. For Wilt's first season, fans swarmed to Allen Fieldhouse, where attendance increased by a whopping 85,000. In Wilt's debut game he didn't disappoint, scoring 52 points and grabbing 31 rebounds.

Chamberlain was finally contained when the Jayhawks were upset on the road by Iowa State 39–37. It seemed Iowa State had figured out one way to beat the Jayhawks: grab the lead and then stall. The loss put KU number two in the polls behind the undefeated North Carolina Tar Heels. Kansas lost one other game in the regular season when Oklahoma edged them out 56–54. Meanwhile, the North Carolina Tar Heels remained the top-ranked team, marching through the regular season undefeated, escaping with multiple narrow victories. Despite their number two ranking, the Jayhawks still entered the NCAA Tournament as the prohibitive favorite.

Behind "Wilt the Stilt," the Jayhawks advanced to the Final Four down the road in Kansas City where they would face two-time defending NCAA champion San Francisco. KU destroyed the Dons, 80–56, to advance to the championship game against undefeated North Carolina. The Tar Heels had squeezed by Michigan State in triple overtime in the semifinals, bringing their record to a perfect 31–0. Everyone figured after surviving such a marathon game, they'd be far too spent to fight KU in the final.

But the Tar Heels were tough, having taken on the personality of their head coach Frank McGuire—the same Frank McGuire who had coached the St. John's team that Kansas, Clyde Lovellette, and Dean Smith had defeated to win the 1952 NCAA title. After losing to KU in '52, McGuire left St. John's, escaping the streets of New York City for the tobacco fields of North Carolina. McGuire replaced Kansas native Tom Scott as head basketball coach. Although Tom Scott had no direct connection to KU, this coaching change put into motion an unprecedented symbiotic basketball relationship between two seemingly unrelated state universities in North Carolina and Kansas. (A coaching swap between the two schools would transpire over the course of the next fifty years in some of the most unimaginable ways possible.)

Considering what was at stake, the 1957 National Championship basketball game between the universities of Kansas and North Carolina still ranks as the greatest college basketball game ever played. After having survived triple overtime in the semifinals, the Tar Heels some way, somehow, found the magic to do it again and defeated the Jayhawks 54–53 in triple overtime.

The loss to Carolina was so devastating that one has to wonder if Harp was ever able to recover. Wilt hadn't. After the 1958 season, one which found Wilt riddled with injuries, it would be another forty years before Chamberlain would set foot on the KU campus. Harp resigned following the 1963–64 season with the program further away from fielding a title contender than it had ever been. It seems that following in the footsteps of Phog Allen had proved to be nearly impossible. Kansas named Harp's assistant Ted Owens as the new head basketball coach.

Without the pressure of following a legend, Ted Owens got off to a promising start. In 1966, just Owens' second year at the helm, the Jayhawks led by JoJo White and Walt Wesley met Texas Western and their coach Don Haskins in the regional final of the NCAA Tournament. At stake was a date in the Final Four. Texas Western featured the first all-black starting five in college basketball history. Although Kentucky had topped the polls, it was Kansas who Haskins feared the most. Said Haskins, "Kansas was the best team we played that year. Better than Kentucky. Whoever won this game was going to win the National Championship."

The highly competitive back and forth affair would go down as one of the greatest games in the history of the NCAA Tournament. After regulation, the score was tied 69 a piece. In overtime, with the score tied at 71, JoJo White hit a jump shot right at the buzzer to seemingly give Kansas the win. But the official made an infamous call, still highly debated today. He claimed White's foot had just grazed the out of bounds line. In the second overtime, Texas Western squeaked out an 81–80 win. They marched on to the title game where they made history by defeating an all-white, Adolph Rupp–coached Kentucky team for the crown.

Despite the heartbreaking defeat, Owens' winning ways continued. In 1971, he had arguably his best team behind stars Dave Robisch and Bud Stallworth. That year KU cruised to a 27–3 record and a perfect 14–0 mark in the Big Eight Conference. The Jayhawks made it to the Final Four where they ultimately lost to the powerhouse UCLA Bruins en route to one of their ten NCAA titles over a twelve-year period.

In his first seven years Ted Owens' KU teams had gone a combined 149–43 and the future looked bright. But the next ten years for Owens and the Jayhawks proved to be up and down. After back-to-back unheard of losing seasons in '72 and '73, KU made it back to the Final Four in 1974 where they lost again in the semifinals, this time to Marquette. From 1975 to 1981, Owens teams won but failed to make a deep postseason run. In '82 and '83, with a young and inexperienced ballclub, for the second time in Owens' tenure, KU had unfathomable

The young instructor James Naismith at Springfield College.

Naismith's classmate and friend, Amos Alonzo Stagg, who would later recommend him for the job at KU.

Dr. Luther Gullick, the Director of the YMCA Training College, who challenged Naismith to come up with a new game.

Photos courtesy of Springfield College Archives

The YMCA School for Christian Workers Building where basketball was invented.

The gymnasium inside the YMCA where the first game of basketball was played.

VOL. I.   JANUARY 15, 1892.   NO. 10.

THE
TRIANGLE

CONTENTS

In the Interest of all-around Physical Education and Recreation.

The YMCA first published the rules of basketball in The Triangle Magazine *just a few weeks after Naismith introduced the game.*

Basket Ball.

The ball to be an ordinary Association foot ball.

1. The ball may be thrown in any direction with one or both hands.

2. The ball may be batted in any direction with one or both hands (never with the fist).

3. A player cannot run with the ball, the player must throw it from the spot on which he catches it, allowance to be made for a man who catches the ball when running at a good speed.

4. The ball must be held in or between the hands, the arms or body must not be used for holding it.

5. No shouldering, holding, pushing, tripping or striking in any way the person of an opponent shall be allowed. The first infringement of this rule by any person shall count as a foul, the second shall disqualify him until the next goal is made, or if there was evident intent to injure the person, for the whole of the game, no substitute allowed.

6. A foul is striking at the ball with the fist, violation of rules 3 and 4, and such as described in rule 5.

7. If either side makes three consecutive fouls it shall count a goal for the opponents (consecutive means without the opponents in the meantime making a foul).

8. A goal shall be made when the ball is thrown or batted from the grounds into the basket and stays there, providing those defending the goal do not touch or disturbe the goal. If the ball rests on the edge and the opponent moves the basket it shall count as a

Page one of James Naismith's Original Rules of Basketball

goal.

9. When the ball goes out of bounds it shall be thrown into the field, and played by the person first touching it. In case of a dispute the umpire shall throw it straight into the field. The thrower in is allowed five seconds, if he holds it longer it shall go to the opponent. If any side presists in delaying the game, the umpire shall call a foul on them.

10. The umpire shall be judge of the men, and shall note the fouls, and notify the referee when three consecutive fouls have been made. He shall have power to disqualify men according to Rule 5.

11. The referee shall be judge of the ball and shall decide when the ball is in play, in bounds, and to which side it belongs, and shall keep the time. He shall decide when a goal has been made, and keep account of the goals with any other duties that are usually performed by a referee.

12. The time shall be two fifteen minutes halves, with five minutes rest between.

13. The side making the most goals in that time shall be declared the winners. In case of a draw the game may, by agreement of the captains, be continued until another goal is made.

First draft of Basket Ball rules.
thing in the gym that the boys might
learn the rules — Dec. 1891 James Naismith
6-28-31.

Page two of James Naismith's Original Rules of Basketball

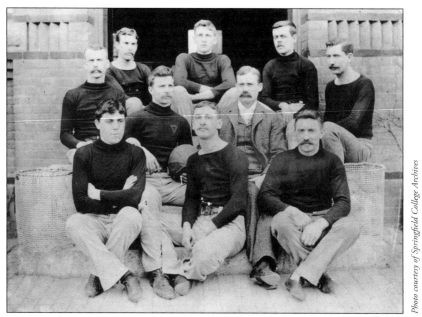

The first basketball team ever assembled at the Springfield YMCA in 1891 (Middle row, right, is James Naismith).

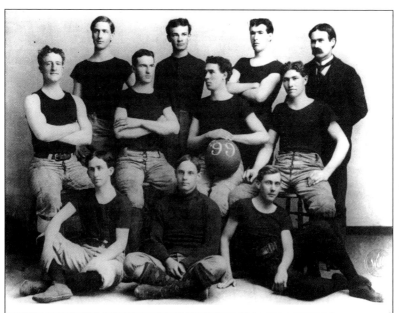

The first Kansas basketball team in 1899 (James Naismith standing, back right).

The 1908 Kansas basketball team (Middle row: Phog Allen second from right/James Naismith second from left).

NATIONAL BASKETBALL CHAMPIONS, 1923

Back Row, l-r: Rupp, Mosby, Ackerman, Wilkins; Second Row, l-r: Wulf,
Dr. F.C. Allen, Dr. Naismith, Black, Frederick; Front Row, l-r: Glaskin,
Bowman, Endicott, McDonald.

Perhaps the most iconic Kansas Basketball picture of all time. The 1923 Helms National Champion team photo featuring Phog Allen middle row second from left, James Naismith to his right. Behind Allen to his right is Adolph Rupp. Front row with ball is basketball Hall of Famer, Paul Endacott.

James Naismith and Phog Allen pose for the camera.

Kansas Coach Phog Allen and his former player, Kentucky Coach Adolph Rupp, pose for a picture.

UNIVERSITY OF KANSAS
Basketball School
1988 National Champions

Me with Coach Larry Brown at Kansas Basketball Camp in 1988.

The Jayhawk shrine at my parent's house in Kansas . . . no wonder I'm crazy!

At the Alamodome in San Antonio just after witnessing 'Mario's Miracle' in 2008. (Left to right: Micah, Smu, myself, Daymion)

Micah and I standing on James Naismith Court in 2011.

Meeting Drew Gooden in Milwaukee.

Interviewing Cole Aldrich in Milwaukee.

Interviewing Jay Bilas of ESPN in Las Vegas.

Watching video testimony with Louise and Mark Allen at their home in Kansas.

Afraid to look while standing behind David and Suzanne Booth during the auction.

Going in for a hug with David Booth after the auction.

With Mom and Dad at the Lawrence premiere of my ESPN 30 for 30 documentary, "There's No Place Like Home."

The Booths and myself at the Lawrence film premiere of the ESPN 30 for 30 documentary, "There's No Place Like Home."

Standing on James Naismith Court in Allen Fieldhouse, telling the faithful that the rules were coming home.

Visiting Naismith's Memorial Park Cemetary in Lawrence, Kansas.

Dr. Naismith's gravestone

back-to-back losing seasons. The Jayhawks hadn't won a conference title in five years. Worst of all, apathy had set in among the fan base. Allen Fieldhouse was no longer an intimidating fortress for opposing teams. Student attendance had waned. Kansas basketball was experiencing something of a down period. At most schools a coach with two Final Fours on his resume would be able to survive two losing seasons. But not at Kansas.

A new athletic director, Monte Johnson, had taken over the reins in Lawrence and felt the need for a fresh start. Johnson had already fired the beloved KU football coach Don Farmbrough, whose program had similarly fallen on hard times. Monte Johnson did the same to Ted Owens, firing him after nineteen years as the head coach of Kansas. Owens' unceremonious exit put a negative spin on a great career. Johnson focused his attention on finding a new coach, as this would be perhaps the most important hire in the history of the program.

Johnson turned to Kansas alum Dean Smith. In twenty-two years as the head coach of North Carolina, Smith had become the most successful coach in the country. He had already taken his Tar Heels to seven Final Fours and just one year previously had won his first National Championship behind a sophomore phenom named Michael Jordan. Smith was still young at just fifty-two years of age and certainly had many quality years ahead of him.

Johnson met with Dean Smith to offer him the position. Dean declined, as Chapel Hill was home for Smith and his family, now more than ever. But he had a suggestion for Johnson. One of his former players, Larry Brown, was coaching the New Jersey Nets of the NBA and Smith had a hunch Brown was ready to return to the college game. Brown had spent two years coaching UCLA before bolting for the Nets.

Johnson met with Brown immediately. Word of the interview reached Nets brass and Brown was quickly given an ultimatum. He was told by owner Joe Taub that he would not be allowed to finish the NBA season before making a decision. Taub wanted to know immediately, "Would it be Kansas or New Jersey?"

The Journey

Friday, December 3: 7 Days Until Auction

The next morning, I arrived back in New York City looking for answers. With the auction only one week away, the exhibit was up at Sotheby's and the public could now come view the rules in person. My plan was to show up at the auction house, unannounced, and put their resident expert, Selby Kiffer, on the spot. Meanwhile, I had arranged for a colleague of mine to meet with Leila Dunbar, a consultant on the auction and one of the industry's foremost experts on sports memorabilia. Between Kiffer and Dunbar, I hoped to settle this authenticity issue once and for all.

After landing at LaGuardia Airport, I had a message from Mark Allen asking me to call him immediately. When I did, he relayed what he had learned from speaking to various people. He explained that there was not merely a singular reason behind the trepidation, but various questions and concerns that needed to be addressed.

The first issue had to do with the fact that other versions of the rules were in circulation, with one being sold a few years prior at the Heritage Auction House in Texas. That version had been sold as an early reproduction, similar to the one hanging in Mark's basement. The hand notations made by Naismith in pen—at the bottom of the rules themselves—included the sentence: "First Draft of Basketball Rules—Hung in the gym so the boys might learn the rules." Naismith then added the date, "February 1892." The version sold at the Heritage Auction House and hanging on the Allen wall had stopped there.

But the version at Sotheby's didn't say "Feb. 1892" after the same handwritten sentence. On Sotheby's offering, the date read "Dec. 1891." If Sotheby's was selling the original, from which these early twentieth century reproductions were made, then why didn't the date on it match the date on the reproductions?

That was issue number one. Issue number two had to do with the seller of the rules himself, Ian Naismith. Little did I know that Ian had something of a checkered past. At times, his relationship with KU had been extremely volatile. He was famously known to be a hothead, and KU's athletic department had often sat at the top of his shit list.

One story had Ian famously demanding KU make yet another donation to his International Basketball Foundation or else, as the story goes, he threatened to have the name "James Naismith" removed from the basketball court. Administrators at KU brushed him off, as Ian had become something of a pest over the years, showing up in Lawrence unannounced with a growing list of demands. Apparently, Ian felt that KU owed him something or at least owed his family something—a debt that in his eyes could never completely be repaid. So KU seemingly stopped trying.

Ian had burned bridges everywhere he'd been. He built a reputation as a bit of an outlaw, gallivanting around town, carrying his gold briefcase with the rules. And what about that gold briefcase? If the rules were worth so much money, why would Ian so nonchalantly carry them around and risk losing them or having them stolen? One story had Ian frantically driving back to an Overland Park, Kansas, Hooters when he thought he had continued on down the highway towards Lawrence without them. Ian was relieved to discover that the gold briefcase had simply slid to the back of the van he was driving.

Just two generations removed from his grandfather, a man who by all accounts was defined by his integrity and morality, ironically stood Ian and his International Basketball Foundation, whose primary mission was to promote good sportsmanship. Ian had operated his Naismith Sportsmanship tour with the help of a local businessman named Keith Zimmerman. The two had been introduced by a mutual friend years prior, and immediately recognized a common ground. Zimmerman was enamored with the brash, outspoken Naismith and his royal basketball bloodline. At the same time, Ian needed a partner to book his appearances and negotiate fees on behalf of his foundation.

It was to bolster the funds of this very foundation that Ian had finally decided to sell the rules, and he charged Zimmerman with finding a suitable buyer, promising him 10 percent of any such deal. In 2005, Zimmerman was able to pique the interest of an individual tied into the tribe leaders of the Indian Gaming Commission. Allegedly, the Indian tribes agreed to pool a whopping $10 million to purchase the rules.

The tribes were seemingly flushed with cash from their various casino holdings throughout the United States. The Indians saw the rules as a way to bring attention to their own proud basketball heritage. Haskell Indian College, located in Lawrence, was known to be an early breeding ground for the game, and Naismith had frequently made trips there to watch them play. Phog Allen had spent time coaching at Haskell as well. With the rules in their possession, the Indians planned to build a shrine to the basketball tradition at Haskell . . . or so the story goes.

The deal required several tribe leaders to dedicate a certain sum to the purchase of the rules until the $10 million was collected. When it was, Ian was asked to do one last thing before the money switched hands: authenticate the rules. Allegedly, Ian felt threatened by such a demand and swiftly backed out of the deal. This begged the question: Why would Ian pull out of a deal worth so much money when all that was left to do was have the rules authenticated?

Not wanting to lead the fight for anything other than the real, original rules of basketball, I hung up with Mark and headed directly to Sotheby's. Upon entering the mammoth building, I found the rules hanging front and center for all to see. Selby Kiffer was there just as I expected. Avi turned on his camera and with Selby, I immediately jumped into the matter at hand. "Can you talk about Sotheby's authentication process?" I began. "Your standpoint is these were the rules that hung in the gym when Naismith invented the game of basketball?"

"There's no doubt these are the rules that hung in the gym," replied Selby. "The paper, the typeface, the handwriting, everything is appropriate for the period of 1891. Beyond that, it's hard to answer specific questions without knowing what those specific questions are, but if there is some thought that what we are offering here is one of those photostatic copies of which several are still in circulation, um . . . you know, that's absurd. I can't put it any other way. There's every reason based on the physical characteristics of the document as well as what we know about the provenance and perhaps most importantly what we know that Dr. Naismith wrote about developing and typing these rules that these are the two sheets that were thumb-tacked to the wall of the gymnasium. You can even see the pin pricks in the corners of the pages where that was done."

After looking at the thumbtack pricks and scanning the document closely, I moved to the date issue. Written in ink at the bottom it said, "Dec. 1891." As I looked closely at the date, something became crystal clear. Behind "Dec. 1891," it clearly used to say "Feb. 1892." The "Feb." had been erased, as had the "2" in "1892." However, both were still clearly visible. I pressed Kiffer for an explanation. "Can you explain this date right here?" I asked. "It's clear that an older date of Feb. 1892 is erased and then a new date of Dec. 1891 is put over that?"

"Well I think, as time went on, Dr. Naismith's memory had a lapse or two, and when he decided that perhaps he should annotate these so people would recognize what they were, he wrote, 'First draft of basketball rules hung in the gym that boys might learn the rules' and initially misremembering, put February 1892. (Soon after the rules were first published in the YMCA's *Triangle Magazine*.) And either when he realized his error or perhaps even had the error pointed out, that (old date) was effaced and the correct date of December 1891 was written in. And then, at a later date he added his name and the date and then he signed it."

Selby's explanation made perfect sense. All of the photostatic copies looked exactly the same, with the date of Feb. 1892. But discovering that the original rules *used to say* Feb. 1892 meant that all of the reproductions were in fact made from this original version.

It occurred to me how many holes the Indian story had. Ian clearly had no issues bringing the rules into one of the world's foremost authenticators in Sotheby's. And even if the story were true, it no longer mattered, as Sotheby's had in fact authenticated the rules. "Are you surprised that there would be those who question the rules' authenticity?" I finally asked Kiffer.

"Well, it actually seems that some people think these might be an early photostatic copy, which on the face of it is absurd. It would be like Sotheby's offering for sale a photograph of a painting and claiming it was an original painting. The obvious distinction is that with a copy, everything is essentially in black and white. On the original rules, there is the annotation at the top "Basket Ball," which is in this late nineteenth century sepia ink and this fountain pen here is clearly blue." [Selby said this while pointing to the phrase "into the basket," which Naismith had written in blue ink after the rules had been typed.]

I looked at the colored ink. This was clearly another validation of Sotheby's offering as all of the photostats were in black and white. On top of that, every single nuanced pen marking, ink drop, and bit of written and typed text perfectly matched between the photostats and Sotheby's version. Without any question, Sotheby's offering was the main source from which Naismith made the photostats for friends and family when he arrived at KU, including the copy in Mark Allen's basement.

Across town, Leila Dunbar's testimony got even more specific in backing up what Selby Kiffer was saying. "When you research and authenticate any item that comes in, you examine several things," she said. "You examine the object itself and with the rules we looked at the paper, we looked at the typescript, we looked at the signature because obviously we want to make sure that it's not a copy. When we research that, and it was a team, it was a number of people, we all unanimously agreed that there were no issues—that the paper was correct, the typescript was correct, the signature was correct, everything matched to what it was supposed to be."

Like Kiffer, Dunbar seemed surprised by the authenticity questions. "This is actually the first time we're hearing of any questioning of the authenticity and it's easy to say, there's no doubt in our minds, there are no red flags at all to debate and therefore, there's no reason to think in any way shape or form they're not what they are. And Sotheby's, just like Christie's and other major auction houses, you know, we pride ourselves on that. I pride myself on that as a consultant, dealing with millions upon millions of dollars of memorabilia on a regular basis. We all put our reputations on the line and we wouldn't do that if there was even a shadow, an iota of a doubt."

While Ian's camp confirmed that the Indian deal had indeed been in the works, they scoffed at the notion that $10 million had ever been raised. After waiting through a never- ending series of empty promises, Ian cut ties with these "jokers." Allegedly, Ian was not about to hand over the rules to anyone without proof that the funds had actually been raised. According to Mike LaChapelle, the "Agent to the Rules," "It's inconceivable that Ian would have backed out of a deal with $10 million on the table. If this group had actually gathered $10 million, Ian would have sold the rules in a heartbeat."

I quickly emailed the authentication testimony of both Selby Kiffer and Leila Dunbar to Deborah Foster and begged her to get it in front of David Booth. She said she would do her best but admitted that David was now rather lukewarm on the whole thing. Deborah's tone had me convinced that I was losing David once and for all. And with only a week until auction day, he seemed to be my only realistic shot, the Jayhawk Nation's only shot at winning this thing. I knew it had to be Booth, his name was already on the building . . . of all the streets in Lawrence, he had grown up on Naismith Drive.

It seemed to me that David needed a reminder of why this was important. My first thought was to try again to get an interview with current Kansas head coach Bill Self or at least to try and get Self to call Booth. I doubted Bill Self even had any idea as to what I was doing. I wondered if he even knew about the auction in the first place. I knew if Self were to back me, it could be a difference maker. But the school had told me in no uncertain terms that they would not be cooperating, thus all contact with Self was essentially cut off. Even if I tried to go around the administration, there was no getting around the fact that the season was well underway—a season which found Self and KU sitting atop the nationwide polls. Clearly, Bill Self had other things on his mind. So I ruled him out for the time being.

But I wondered about some of the other coaches. As I saw it, this entire mission was very much about the head coaches at Kansas. After all, in nearly 115 years of basketball, only eight men had sat in the head-coaching chair at the university, and Naismith had been the first. It was that very lineage—that legacy—that I was trying to honor and hold intact. So I thought of the coaches I grew up with, Larry Brown and Roy Williams. As luck would have it, Williams and Brown lived right down the road from each other in North Carolina. I wondered where they would think the rules of basketball belonged? Would they agree with me? If they were to back me up, perhaps it would reinvigorate David Booth. But could I even get to these guys?

I crafted an email to both coaches and called my colleague, talent booker Jen Aiello, who forwarded the requests to the appropriate administrators. Both coaches' liaisons wrote back immediately and said they'd be happy to see me. With those meetings confirmed, I immediately booked some plane tickets and set off for North Carolina, on the hunt for a couple Hall of Fame coaches.

9

THE MESSIAH

GROWING UP, I would often be reminded of the Jewish pitching great Sandy Koufax of the Brooklyn and Los Angeles Dodgers. Koufax made history when he refused to pitch Game 1 of the 1965 World Series because it fell on Yom Kippur. With that decision Koufax became forever cemented atop the pantheon of Jewish American sports heroes. For here was not just a dominant player on the field, but a man defined by his integrity and fully committed to his faith.

But I for one was tired of hearing about Sandy Koufax. Koufax was long before my time. Koufax was my father's hero. As a child obsessed with sports, I spanned the professional and college ranks. Aside from ownership and executives in the front office, there were no Jews to be found. Long gone were the days of the "Underground Railroad," where Jews like Lennie Rosenbluth and Art Heyman dominated college hoops. The heyday of Eddie Gottlieb and the great South Philadelphia Hebrew squads were now a distant memory. The New York

Knickerbockers of Ossie Schectman (who scored the first NBA basket), Sonny Hertzberg, Stan Stutz, Hank Rosenstein, and Leo Gottlieb seemed to be from some other distant universe where Jewish people excelled playing basketball.

Even the Jewish coaching greats were a thing of the past. Nat Holman who led CUNY to the 1950 National Championship, Red Auerbach who orchestrated the Boston Celtics dynasty in the 1950s and '60s, and Red Holzman, who led the New York Knicks to NBA titles in '70 and '73. As I surveyed the world of sports I wondered, where was my hero?

On Friday, April 8, 1983, I found him. His name was Lawrence Harvey Brown; a Brooklyn-born, Long Island–bred Jew who was named the sixth head coach in Kansas basketball history. Brown had chosen Kansas instead of New Jersey. "I wouldn't have considered just any job," Brown said. "Kansas is special. It had to be a special job."

And so the Kansas/North Carolina relationship continued. We had sent our prodigal son Dean Smith out east where he'd made Carolina Blue synonymous with college basketball excellence. Dean had rebutted our request for his return but instead he sent his very best protégé our way. "My college coach is from Kansas," Brown said at his introductory press conference. "He always talked to me about Kansas, the tradition, atmosphere, and history."

In Brown's first two years, the Jayhawks were eliminated in the Sweet Sixteen. They had been good. They were getting ready to be great. With sophomore star Danny Manning joining upperclassmen like Ron Kellogg, Calvin Thompson, Greg Deiling, and Cedric Hunter, KU was a deep, experienced team with talent at every position. As such, the Jayhawks ran away with the Big Eight conference and postseason tournament, finishing 30–3 and earning a #1 seed in the 1986 NCAA Tournament.

After squeezing by Michigan State in the Sweet Sixteen, KU beat North Carolina State in the Elite Eight to advance to their first Final Four in twelve seasons. KU would face Johnny Dawkins and the #1-seeded Duke Blue Devils in the national semifinal.

The game would be tight throughout. Kansas pulled ahead for a 65–61 lead with just over four minutes left. But Duke's defense went into high gear, holding Kansas to a single basket the rest of the game. Danny Ferry scored on a rebound to give Duke a 69–67 lead and the Blue Devils ended up winning the game 71–67. Johnny Dawkins finished with a game high 24 points for the Blue Devils while KU's star, Danny Manning, was held to just 4 points, 13 below his season average.

Duke went on to lose to Louisville in the National Championship game. Meanwhile the Jayhawks' star Danny Manning, who was projected to be a can't miss NBA lottery pick, professed his undying commitment to Kansas. To the delight of KU fans, Manning returned for his junior season, one in which the Jayhawks would lose to Georgetown in the Sweet Sixteen. When Manning also returned for his senior season, KU fans similarly felt grateful for one more year to watch one of the greatest players in Kansas basketball history.

When the 1988 season began, there was reason for optimism. With Manning we knew we'd have the best player in every game we played and thus a legitimate chance to win every game we played. But twenty games through the season, it seemed our optimism had been misguided. Coming off four straight losses KU was 12–8 overall and 1–4 in the Big Eight conference. Forget the NCAA Tournament, we wondered if an NIT invite was even in the cards. But the Jayhawks regrouped to go 9–3 over their last 12 games and finish the season at 21–11. They had done just enough to earn an at-large bid and a number six seed in the NCAA Tournament.

1988 marked the fiftieth anniversary of the NCAA Tournament. As a testament to the past and to commemorate the occasion, the NCAA had chosen Kansas City's Kemper Arena as the site of the Final Four. But '88 was also a testament to the future. The NCAA knew that March Madness had finally, once and for all, captivated the nation. They knew that the demand to attend the event far outweighed the supply of available tickets. They understood by playing in 20,000-capacity arenas they were leaving behind loads of potential revenue. So in 1988 in Kansas City, there would be one last Final Four in an intimate setting, before the era of the mammoth domes began.

When the tournament began, we didn't allow ourselves to entertain the possibility of a magical Final Four run that would land the Hawks just down the road in Kansas City. Based on KU's play over the course of the year, such a run seemed totally and completely inconceivable. Sure we had the best player in the country, but there were absolute behemoths out there, the most imposing of which was from our own conference, the Oklahoma Sooners who'd beaten us twice already that year.

Winning the first round game against Xavier was not surprising as the Jayhawks were seeded higher than the Musketeers. Then KU caught a break when #3 seed North Carolina State had been upset by the #14 seed Murray State. Kansas squeezed by Murray State 61–58 to face another Cinderella in Vanderbilt, who'd upset the #2 seed Pittsburgh. KU got by Vanderbilt, setting up an Elite Eight matchup against in-state rival Kansas State. Though K-State was the higher seed, for a rivalry game such as this, records could be thrown out the window. The winner would have the luxury of playing in the Final Four just down the road in Kansas City.

Kansas was able to beat K-State and advance to their second Final Four in three seasons. As thrilled as we were, we tempered our excitement knowing that three basketball giants would be joining us in Kansas City. In one matchup the Oklahoma Sooners would be facing the Arizona Wildcats. The winner of that game would face the winner of Kansas and Duke. After the heartbreaking loss in 1986, we'd finally get another shot at the Blue Devils.

Maybe the stars had aligned? Maybe in this, the last Final Four in Kansas City, the ghosts of Naismith and Allen were orchestrating a miracle run for the ages? Maybe it was time to start thinking we had a shot to win this thing? At the very least maybe we should consider scalping tickets to attend the game? I went to my dad and proposed that we make an effort to go.

"No," said my dad. At thirteen years of age, though I had recently had my bar mitzvah and was considered by my faith to be a man, I was in fact not a man. I was a child who desperately, more than anything in the world, wanted the Jayhawks to win a title, and I wanted to see them do it in person. My dad was undoubtedly a man and as far as the Jayhawks were concerned, he was in charge. And he made his standpoint crystal clear: We would not begin to entertain winning this game as we still had to play the best team in the country—a team stacked with players Stacey King, Harvey Grant, Mookie Blaylock, and Ricky Grace—a team that had already beaten us twice that same year. My dad maintained that on the outside chance we kept the game close, we would not deviate from watching the game in our family room, where we had been 5–0 in the tournament thus far.

On Saturday, April 2nd, we readied for our game with Duke. Six weeks earlier the Blue Devils had come into Allen Fieldhouse for a regular season match up. In that game, the Jayhawks had rolled out to a 23–8 lead, only to see Duke mount a remarkable comeback and win in overtime.

Ten minutes into the national semifinal, Kansas again jumped out on Duke to take a 24–6 lead. But considering what had transpired in Lawrence, we waited for the Blue Devils to respond and take the lead . . . but they didn't. Kansas hung on for a 66–59 victory and Danny Manning was able to avenge the Final Four loss that had left him devastated two years prior. Now somehow, someway the Cinderella Jayhawks would be facing the Oklahoma Sooners the following Monday night for the National Championship.

That Monday at school felt like an eternity. Every minute seemed like an hour, every hour a day. When the ref finally brought the ball to center court, it felt like I'd woken up a week ago. But once the ball went in the air, the game flew by, like none I'd ever witnessed.

The first half of the 1988 Championship Game was a dizzying back and forth affair. Oklahoma was everything they had been touted to be. Their 3-point specialist Dave Sieger couldn't miss. But neither could the Jayhawks. For the first twenty minutes, KU managed to stay right with Oklahoma, running their own version of fast break basketball. At halftime of the fiftieth anniversary of the NCAA Tournament, the score was tied 50–50.

Although we were extremely fortunate to be tied at the half, we felt out of our comfort zone. Kansas hadn't scored 50 in a half all season long. Meanwhile, Oklahoma had averaged 103.5 points per game. They were deeper, quicker, built to go fast for 40 minutes. So at halftime, we still entertained no grand illusions of victory and instead waited for the inevitable collapse to come.

With twelve minutes to go, Kansas trailed 65–60. It seemed the Sooners would finally pull away and win. But then something happened. Throughout the game thus far, Larry Brown had subbed in what seemed like the entire KU bench, bringing in even the most seldom used players to play meaningful minutes. The Sooners on the other hand had stuck with their core group for the entire game. As such, with 10 minutes to play, it was the Sooners who looked tired, not the Jayhawks. It seemed Brown and KU had run with OU by intelligent design.

The fresher Jayhawks fought back to tie the game. On offense, KU began to spread it out, slow the pace down, and run the shot clock. With 5:30 to go, Kevin Pritchard hit a leaner to give KU a 73–71 lead. Oklahoma still appeared exhausted. Their star center Stacey King had been almost unheard of in the second half, while his counterpart Danny Manning was everywhere on the court.

With 3:05 to go, Chris Piper swished a shot to give KU its biggest lead of the game at 77–71. OU fought back, cutting the lead to 78–77 with 40 seconds left. With 16 seconds remaining Oklahoma fouled Scooter Barry, the son of NBA great Rick Barry. Scooter made the first before missing the second. But Danny Manning grabbed a huge rebound and was immediately fouled again. Manning stepped to the line and made both shots to give the Jayhawks an 81–77 edge with 14 seconds left. Oklahoma's Ricky Grace raced down the court and scored a layup and cut the lead to 81–79. With just five seconds to go, Danny Manning was fouled. He stepped to the line with a chance to ice it for the Jayhawks.

Among a paranoid group of fans gathered inside our home, I couldn't believe what I was watching unfold. The entire game had seemed like some sort of dream sequence. Kansas had played the perfect game. And now, somehow, Danny Manning, perhaps the greatest Jayhawk of all time, was stepping to the line with a chance to ice a National Championship. Danny Manning, who had turned down NBA fame and fortune to return to KU, was on the verge of delivering the most remarkable championship in Jayhawk history.

Manning's first attempt rattled in. One more and the title was ours! His second shot went up and fell straight through the nylon. Oklahoma threw up a meaningless shot as time expired. And just like that, it was over. It was over. Over! The fans around me exploded. I turned to find my dad. He had waited his entire life for this, religiously following the Jayhawks like an obsessed lunatic, turning his oldest son into the same. And now in our finest moment, I assumed we'd come together in an epic embrace. After years of disappointment, in this legendary grasp all of it would seem worth it, necessary growing pains to truly appreciate this moment. But when I finally located him he was too far ahead of me to reach. In front of a packed house of neighbors and friends and relatives, he had already taken off his shirt and ran around the house screaming, "National Champions! National Champions! National Champions!" I just laughed, dizzy with ecstasy, and wondered . . . had I just witnessed a miracle?

The Journey

Monday, December 6: 4 Days Until Auction

While the world continues to wait patiently for the Messiah, Kansas fans experienced him firsthand. He came in the form of a Jewish boy from New York named Larry Brown, who descended upon Lawrence and swiftly returned it to the basketball promised land it once was. In five glorious years, Brown had rebuilt the first temple of hoops, and a light once again shone through the stained glass windows of Allen Fieldhouse.

Kansas' impossible run further perpetuated Brown's reputation as a whiz-kid coaching prodigy, an x-and-o mastermind with an uncanny ability to pull more out of less than anyone in basketball. Brown was unmistakably Jewish, with his dark features, dark-rimmed glasses, and slow, contemplative drawl. All at once he looked like my rabbi, my father, and my pediatrician. His over-analytic, glass-half-empty outlook seemed distinctly Jewish too. Known to be a perfectionist and impossibly hard on his players, Brown was notoriously discontented. After winning the title in '88, Brown admitted that for the first time in his coaching life, he was actually happy and able to enjoy events of the moment. And I for one hoped his happiness would last. I prayed that my hero would stay put in Lawrence and wouldn't continue on his nomadic basketball quest.

But where there is work to do, where there are people suffering, the healer is beckoned. The pattern is never-ending. Once the sick are restored to health, it's on to the next one. Such a calling would come to define the career of "next town Larry Brown."

In Texas, there were people suffering; a franchise and their fans were in desperate need of help. The San Antonio Spurs had decided that Larry Brown was the only one who could resuscitate them, and they were willing to pay him a ton of money to do so. So after returning Kansas to prominence, Brown shockingly bolted Lawrence and returned to the NBA, where he would remain for another twenty-two years, eventually becoming the only coach in history to win both an NCAA and an NBA title.

Shortly after the devastating news of Larry's departure, my family and I attended a spring fundraiser at the K. I. Synagogue in Overland Park, Kansas. As I wandered aimlessly around the temple festivities, I was amazed to find a shiny new basketball up for raffle. This was no ordinary basketball. In black marker written on the ball were the words, "1988 National Champions." Under these words, also in black marker, the ball was signed, "Best Wishes, Larry Brown." Raffle tickets were being sold for $1, so I bought a ticket, wrote my name and phone number, and put it in the canister holding hundreds of others.

At home that night, I sat patiently by the phone waiting for it to ring. I just knew it would. It finally did. I picked it up on one ring. "Hello," the voice on the other end said "this is Suzy from K. I., is Josh Swade there?"

Twenty-two years later, as I walked into the Time Warner Cable Arena to meet with Larry Brown, I thought about that ball sitting in my parents' house. Brown had made many stops since he had signed that ball. In his illustrious career, he had been the consummate nomad, coaching a total of fourteen teams. Brown had been basketball's version of "the wandering Jew." As I traversed the country trying to get Naismith's rules to Kansas, I felt like a wandering Jew myself. And I was starting to wonder if Brown was as confused about home as I was. Was my home in Kansas where I was born and raised? Or was my home in New York where I'd lived for over fifteen years?

"Can you talk about home?" I asked him. "What does home mean to you?"

"Well, home has been a lot of different places," said Brown. "When I coached the Knicks, my home was New York. When I coached Philly, my home was Philly. When I coached Kansas, my home was Kansas. The one thing that separates Kansas from so many other places is when you're the coach there, you're almost bigger than life. And as a coach you realize how important your position is to so many people. And I don't think people get any better than in the Midwest. Their values are the values I think our sport is really made of. So, when they say there's no place like home . . . I don't think there's a better place to live—or a better place to play basketball or a better place to coach—than the University of Kansas."

"Only eight coaches in 115 years," I said. "That's pretty incredible. What's it like to be part of that small group?"

"Well, you know, I've obviously moved around. But I've always looked at myself as a college coach. And when you coach Kansas, you're part of the community, part of the state. You understand the responsibility you have because so many people care about what's gone on before; and hopefully what's going to go on after. So to be one of those eight coaches, for that program, it doesn't get any better than that."

"If it was so great, why did you leave?"

"It mostly was family related," said Brown. "It had nothing to do with my job. I loved it [there], I loved every minute of it. Hindsight's always better. It's something I look back on and say 'hey man, that [staying] would have been pretty special.'

But, that being said, look who followed me. You know, Roy came in, did an amazing job. And now they got a guy [in Bill Self] who I don't think there's a better coach in our sport, or a better person. And that's why I think our program is in such good hands."

"When Bill Self was introduced as coach, he said, speaking of you, here's a guy that played and coached at North Carolina and coached at UCLA. And you said, those places are great, but they're not Kansas. What did you mean by that?"

"Well, you're going to get me in a lot of trouble," said Brown, smiling wide. "But I mean, obviously, UCLA, when you consider what they did, with Coach Wooden being there, Lew Alcindor; that's phenomenal. Nobody is going to win the championships they won in such short amount of time. And Chapel Hill, when you consider Coach [Dean] Smith and players like Michael Jordan. But Kansas . . . Kansas it's like . . . it's almost like a religion. I remember the first time as coach I walked into Allen, and I walked around the stands. People were at the game that were there when Coach Allen was there. Season ticket holders for fifty years."

When Larry brought up religion, I couldn't help but bring up mine. "Speaking of religion. I'm Jewish, and I'm from Kansas. So you were like The Messiah in my family. What was it like for you being Jewish in Kansas?"

"You know, I never really thought about it. When I was growing up . . . I grew up in a town that was almost 80 percent Jewish. And years and years ago, basketball was a Jewish sport, because it evolved out of the inner city. And there were so many Jewish people that had migrated from the old country to the inner city."

"Coach, do you think it's really a coincidence that shortly after my bar mitzvah, after I gave a stirring Torah rendition, we won a miraculous National Championship in 1988?"

"Well, if your bar mitzvah was anything like mine, there's no coincidence. When I was bar mitzvah'd, we had a hurricane. And the rabbi blamed it on me because I didn't study hard enough."

Larry and I laughed like two old yentas telling jokes at the local deli. But it was time to get serious. "At our bar mitzvahs, we received God's commandments, but what do you think about the basketball commandments [Naismith's rules] coming up for auction here in a few days?"

"Well, when I got to see them for the first time, it was amazing. On two pieces of paper. I understand the significance of it. You know, this game has been good to me. I think it's the greatest game ever invented. And the fact that Naismith was at the University of Kansas and was a big part of the tradition at Kansas, I wish the rules of the game would be there on display. Because you talk about the greatest place to play basketball; I don't think it gets any better than Allen Fieldhouse and the University of Kansas. When you walk in there, you see Adolph Rupp, Dean Smith, Wilt Chamberlain, John McClendon, I mean it goes on and on . . . and Naismith started it all. So hopefully somebody will step up and get those simple rules to the university."

I thanked Coach Brown profusely and then floated out of the arena on yet another spiritual high. Coach Brown had preached my gospel right back at me. Now as we headed down the highway to Chapel Hill, I was hoping that Roy Williams would do the same.

10

THE RESURRECTION

WHEN ROY WILLIAMS was announced as the seventh coach in the nearly 100-year history of Kansas basketball, we, the Jayhawk faithful, seemed to come together and collectively scream at the top of our lungs . . . "Who?!"

Not only were we forced to deal with the fact that we hadn't landed a star coach, we had to come to grips with the prospects of a complete and utter unknown, a man whose name had never been mentioned in the swirling rumor mill of potential candidates, a man who elicited no feeling of excitement, no sense that order had been restored.

On July 8, 1988, athletic director Bob Frederick introduced Roy Williams at a press conference. Williams marked the second former Tar Heel to be named the head basketball coach at Kansas in five years. "My hope is you don't have to go through the process of hiring another basketball coach for thirty years," Williams told the media that day.

By no fault of his own, Williams' tenure got off to a disastrous start. In October of 1988, before he had ever coached a game at Kansas, the NCAA released findings that violations had occurred under the watch of Larry Brown, the most severe of which found the previous coach guilty of giving a basketball prospect plane fare to visit his ailing grandmother. As a result, the basketball program would lose three scholarships and not be allowed to have recruits visit campus for an entire year. But worst of all, KU would not be eligible to participate in the post-season tournament in Williams' first year, meaning the Jayhawks would become the first National Champion in NCAA history not eligible to defend their title.

Despite a cloud of negativity hovering over the team due to the NCAA sanctions, the Jayhawks fought hard all year long. Kansas finished a respectable 19–12 overall and Williams clearly had the admiration of his players. His unwillingness to make excuses was beginning to earn him the fans' respect as well.

In 1990, Williams' second year at the helm, KU was picked to finish dead last in the Big Eight. However, behind the emergence of freshman point guard Adonis Jordan and big man Mark Randall, KU would finish 30–5 overall and second in the Big Eight conference. Despite a 1-point loss to UCLA in the NCAA Tournament's second round, the overachieving season had helped Williams silence all doubters. There was no longer any question. Two years at the helm had proven that Roy Williams could indeed coach basketball.

But it was his third year that signified he might in fact be a coaching star. In 1991, KU won the conference championship and entered the NCAA Tournament a #3 seed. After upsetting Indiana and Arkansas, the Jayhawks advanced all the way to the Final Four, where Williams would face his alma mater, the powerhouse North Carolina Tar Heels.

This game would set the stage for a defining moment in KU history. In this matchup, seemingly scripted by some crafty network television executive, Williams was pitted against his mentor Dean Smith, a man he still referred to as "Coach," a man whom without, he would not be here in the first place. This game also pitted Jayhawk fans against one of their own in Smith, a man who had rebuffed appeals for his own return to Mount Oread, a man who had played an integral role in KU's two national titles, but a man who now stood squarely between the Jayhawks and their third. Perhaps never in school history was there a game that KU fans wanted to win more.

The Jayhawks ended the first half on a remarkable 24–6 run carrying a 9-point lead into halftime. Kansas took their momentum into the second half and had the game in control when Dean Smith, with his team trailing 76–71, was ejected for leaving the coach's box. Before heading to the locker room, Smith graciously came down to the Jayhawk bench to congratulate Roy and the entire KU team. As he left the court, the outcome of the game safely in the win column for KU, the Jayhawk faithful felt a deep sense of satisfaction.

We prepared to play the Duke Blue Devils for the NCAA title. Duke had just come off their own upset of UNLV. All season long, KU had used its lack of size to its advantage against teams. The Jayhawks were quicker to the ball and their ability to outrebound a bigger UNC front line proved to be the difference in the previous game. But Duke had speed too, and KU struggled to find any momentum throughout the National Championship game. The Blue Devils ended up winning 72–65, capturing their first NCAA Championship in the process.

When the following season began, any thought that the letdown from the NCAA title loss would carry over was quickly done away with. KU again won the conference and entered the tournament as a #1 seed. But in the second round, the Jayhawks were shockingly upset by Texas El Paso. In 1993, KU again won the conference and advanced to yet another Final Four. The Jayhawks would once again face Dean Smith and the North Carolina Tar Heels.

This time UNC controlled the game and won 78–68. The following Monday, Roy Williams attended the title game and joined the Carolina fans in the stands to cheer on his mentor Dean Smith as he captured his second national title.

In 1995, Kansas once again entered the tournament as a #1 seed and a prohibitive favorite to win it all. But in the Sweet Sixteen, the Jayhawks were upset by the #4-seeded Virginia Cavaliers. With this loss, paranoia began to creep into our minds. One couldn't help but notice a recurring pattern taking shape. Kansas had continually turned in remarkable regular seasons only to lose to lower-seeded teams in the NCAA Tournament. When the Jayhawks lost again to the lower-seeded Syracuse Orange in 1996, our worst fears seemed to be confirmed: the Jayhawks had turned into choke artists of sorts.

If the two previous years had raised our tournament paranoia to new heights, the 1997 Jayhawk squad seemed to be just the prescription we needed; for here was as talented a team ever assembled in Lawrence. The fruit of Roy Williams' tireless recruiting efforts were now fully realized. Our star point guard Jacque Vaughn was joined in the backcourt by deadly outside shooter Jerod Haase. At the wing was Paul Pierce, a smooth California native who had "superstar" written all over him. Our frontcourt was comprised of two highly skilled big men in Raef LaFrentz and Scott Pollard. Despite whatever pressure situations the tournament was sure to present, it appeared that this was a group with simply too much skill to lose to a lesser team.

The media unanimously agreed, and the Jayhawks entered the season as the number one team in the nation. KU rattled off 22 straight wins, blowing away the competition at every instance. A last-second overtime loss at Missouri would prove to be KU's only slipup, and perhaps the greatest team in Kansas basketball history entered the 1997 NCAA Tournament as the overall number one seed with a record of 32–1.

The Jayhawks easily advanced to the Sweet Sixteen to face the #4 seed Arizona Wildcats. Arizona posed little threat and we assumed they would simply be the next victim in a long string of easy defeats. After all, we had our sights set on more serious contenders: the other number one seeds, Kentucky, Carolina, and Minnesota, who were all advancing with relative ease.

But Kansas came out of the gate looking tight as Arizona jumped out to a 12-5 lead. By halftime, the Wildcats had a 2-point lead.

When the second half began, Arizona maintained a small advantage with the Jayhawks seemingly on the verge of taking charge. Then the bottom fell out. Arizona's backcourt duo of Mike Bibby and Miles Simon began raining in threes from all over the court. The entire Arizona team suddenly could not miss a shot. The 'Cats lead quickly grew to 13 with a little over three minutes to play.

Kansas made a valiant comeback, even having a chance to tie the game as time expired. When Raef LaFrentz's last second heave clanked off the rim, it signified perhaps one of the most painful losses in Kansas history.

I tried to approach the 1998 campaign with a grain of salt. I tried to not get my hopes up. I tried to remind myself that we had just stormed through several years of dominating basketball, without a title to show for it. But by the time the tournament rolled around, the #1 seeded Jayhawks looked like the best team yet again. Still, in the second round, an old familiar scenario played out. KU, facing #8 seed Rhode Island, once again made headlines as the tournament's biggest victim, falling 80–75 in a shocking upset.

The Jayhawks lost stars Paul Pierce and Raef LaFrentz to the NBA lottery, and KU finally entered rebuilding mode. Then things got worse. Roy Williams' mentor, Dean Smith, had retired as head coach at North Carolina three years prior. Taking his place had been his longtime trusty aide Bill Guthridge. Guthridge, too, was getting older and had suddenly decided to step down as head coach. So the Tar Heels did what the whole world expected them to do. They quickly offered the job to Roy Williams and with it a chance to return home to Chapel Hill.

In his twelve seasons at Kansas, Roy Williams had emerged as one of the best coaches in basketball. Despite some painful tournament exits, his teams had won more games than any other program during the same time period. It seemed that almost every year another NBA team was aggressively pursuing him with huge offers. Each and every time, Williams said no. Williams wouldn't discuss the various employment opportunities that came across his desk, but his allegiance to KU was summed up best when he said, "right in that building, [Allen

Fieldhouse], is the best place to play and coach in college basketball. I truly believe that."

The Carolina overture was different and we all knew it. Williams had been born and raised in North Carolina. He had spent his entire life there before coming to the University of Kansas. His family still lived there. It didn't take a genius to understand that this would be an offer Roy Williams would have to seriously consider.

News broke that Roy had decided to visit Chapel Hill to investigate the possibility of returning. Meanwhile, back in Lawrence, the Roy Williams "stay" campaign was in full swing. Fans had adorned every entrance to Allen Fieldhouse with some type of visible signage begging Roy Williams to remain in Lawrence. Carolina's fan response was simple and to the point. One person hung a sign on the Dean Dome that read, "Roy, please come home."

Camera crews found Williams arriving back to Lawrence looking haggard, the decision clearly weighing heavily on him. "The last seven days have been the most difficult of my life," he said. "I have people at both places I care a great deal about. I wish I could coach both places."

But he could only choose one. Roy thought about his team at KU and the players he would potentially be leaving behind. The Jayhawks were going to be much improved the following year. A young core of Kirk Hinrich, Drew Gooden, and Nick Collison had shown great promise. Roy thought about those young kids and how hurt they'd be if he left. Roy thought more about Nick Collison. As he wavered back and forth with his decision, he kept coming back to the promise he had made the star prospect before he arrived to KU. Roy promised that he would coach the young man for his entire career. Coach Williams loved Kansas. He loved his players. He was a man of his word. And he ultimately decided, he couldn't break that promise to Nick Collison.

On Thursday, July 6, 2001, after a week of back-and-forth rumors, Williams held a press conference inside Memorial Stadium in Lawrence. In front of 17,000 fans Williams cozied up to the microphone and simply said, "I'm staying." The football stadium shook with a thunderous applause seldom known to a football stadium on the KU campus. Back in Chapel Hill, the local television station that had aired the press conference returned to its regularly scheduled programming.

With Roy staying in Lawrence, we were certain glory was just around the corner. It was time for him to finally win a title and cap off what was sure to be a Hall of Fame career. In 2002, it seemed like a prime opportunity when Kansas once again entered the tournament as a #1 seed and marched all the way to the Final Four.

In the semifinal game KU faced the Maryland Terrapins, also a one seed, and also coached by another Williams, Gary, also looking for his first title. KU jumped out to a 13–2 lead with just over sixteen minutes left in the first half. Maryland called timeout, regrouped, and then slowly and methodically took control of the game. They finished the half on a 42–24 run to take a 7-point lead into the locker room. The Jayhawks ended up losing and Maryland went on to defeat Indiana in the final.

The loss to Maryland meant that Kansas had let five number one seeds over the course of the previous ten years slip by without a title to show for them. Those teams were some of the greatest teams in Jayhawk history, with players like Paul Pierce, Raef LaFrentz, Jacque Vaughn, and Drew Gooden. After the title game, the topic of discussion on ESPN quickly turned to the following season. Dick Vitale made no attempt to downplay his prediction. "Next year," he said, "It will be Rock Chalk Jayhawk."

When the '03 season began, Vitale's prediction seemed to have merit. Frontcourt bruisers Jeff Graves and Wayne Simien would fit along nicely with guards Aaron Miles and Keith Langford. But this team would go as far as their senior leaders would take them. Two Iowa natives, Nick Collison and Kirk Hinrich, had chosen to return to school and delay their inevitable NBA careers to lead KU.

The Jayhawks won the Big 12 and advanced to the NCAA Final Four to take on Marquette and their star Dwyane Wade. As if Wade wasn't enough to worry about, suddenly the prospect of losing Roy Williams to North Carolina reared its ugly head . . . again. Matt Doherty, who had taken the job three years prior, had just been fired by UNC. Doherty's brash style had never caught on in Chapel Hill and after an 8–19 season, he had lost the faith of the players and fans alike. The national sports media once again focused on Roy Williams and Carolina's inevitable pursuit of him. Roy did his best not to discuss the situation in the media, instead focusing on the task at hand.

Any thought that the Carolina talk had posed a distraction for the KU players was quickly eliminated once the semifinal game got underway. The Jayhawks played beautifully, smothering the Golden Eagles and Dwyane Wade, while running all up and down the court. Kansas ended up winning the lopsided affair by 33 points.

With the way KU had dismantled Marquette, it was hard to imagine a scenario where the Jayhawks would not be cutting down the nets on that following Monday night. All that was left to do was get by the surprise #4-seeded Syracuse Orangemen and their freshman phenom, Carmelo Anthony.

But once again, it wasn't meant to be. Behind guard Gerry McNamara, Syracuse came out on fire, making a total of 10 3-pointers in the first half. The Orange took an 11-point lead into the locker room. The Jayhawks fought back valiantly and even had a chance to tie the game until Syracuse's Hakim Warrick swatted KU's Michael Lee's 3-point shot attempt just before time expired. Once again, Kansas had lost a tournament game they had no business losing. The Jayhawks had lost by 3 points. They had missed 18 free throws on the night. 18.

The Journey

Tuesday, December 7: 3 Days Until Auction

In 2003, after KU lost in the National Championship to Syracuse, I sat in the stands of the Superdome in New Orleans, crushed. To add insult to injury, rumors ran wild that Coach Roy Williams would leave Kansas and head home to North Carolina. After the loss outside the KU locker room, Williams famously told CBS reporter Bonnie Bernstein that he "could give a shit about North Carolina right now."

As it turns out, Roy did give a shit. Despite fifteen years at KU, Roy chose to return to North Carolina. For him, Chapel Hill was home. So as I walked into the Carolina basketball offices looking for an endorsement on the rules, I was hoping if anyone would understand what I was trying to do for my home, it would be Ol' Roy.

"What does home mean to Roy Williams?" I began.

Roy thought for a moment, looked me right in the eye, and responded earnestly. "Home is a place you trust people. It's a place where you have that passion to be. And it's a place where you can realize your dreams. For fifteen years, Allen Fieldhouse was home. My office was home. Kansas basketball was home. There were just a lot of extenuating circumstances that changed that."

"Do you think home can be in two places?"

"Well, Chancellor Moeser, my first chancellor here at North Carolina, knew how badly I was struggling with the decision, and he said, you know, it's not immoral to love two institutions. And I did love two institutions. I have my roots as a basketball coach with the University of Kansas. But I have my roots as an individual in North Carolina."

"What's different about basketball here in North Carolina versus basketball in Kansas?"

"You know, there are just so many similarities. I told Coach [Dean] Smith one time, I said, the crazy thing is that the people in Kansas don't know what we have at North Carolina. And the people in North Carolina don't know what we have in Kansas. But all the time I go back to the biggest difference is I think that the people in Kansas take their passion to a level that's unsurpassed. The passion that they watch the games with, the enthusiasm that they watch the games with, it's unmatched. They feel that ownership from Dr. Naismith, through Doc Allen, Larry Brown, all the way down the road. Some other places feel that as well. You know, North Carolina, Kentucky, UCLA. But I do believe that the people at Kansas feel it with more passion than anyone else."

"And obviously the place that passion lives is the place called Allen Fieldhouse. Can you talk to me about Allen Fieldhouse?"

"It's the greatest venue for a college athletic event I've ever been in," said Williams, much to my surprise. "Bar none. You walk in the building and you feel the excitement. And that's impossible. You see the pressure, and that's impossible. But it's true. I used to say sometimes you could cut out a hole through the pressure and excitement in front of you—you needed to be able to do that to see the game. And I honestly felt sometimes that the crowd was not going to let the other team be successful. You had to be careful that they didn't try to make you go too fast or try too many things. I used to talk to my team about using that energy to play defense. But Allen Fieldhouse, the guy that sits on the last row is just as enthusiastic as the student that stands on the first row."

"And you obviously coach in a great place, but there's nothing like it?"

"Nothing like it," he said. "It bothers me right now because I would like to say that we're like it, and our people are really good. We really do some great things. But there's only one Allen Fieldhouse."

"When these rules come up for auction on December 10, where do you think they belong?" I finally asked.

"There's no question in my mind, I'd like to see them back at the University of Kansas. I think that would be the neat thing— the right thing to have happen. I've lived my life trying to decide that things should happen because it's the right thing to happen. And I think this is the right thing to happen for those rules to be back in Allen Fieldhouse on Naismith Drive—that's where I think they should be."

And just like that, I was completely and forever at peace with Coach Williams and his decision to return home to North Carolina.

Back at the hotel, I emailed the best moments from both coach's interviews over to Deborah Foster. She promised me she would get the footage in front of David Booth. I then sent the footage to Mark Allen and called him on the phone. With only one week until the auction, I told him he had to come to Austin to help me get Booth back on board. It was becoming increasingly clear that if we had any chance to win this auction, David Booth was our only shot.

"I can't go to Austin," said Mark. "There's just no way. I'm swamped at work and I have a medical conference in Florida next week. You don't need me."

I told Mark he was wrong, that I absolutely needed him. I told him that he offered many things I didn't have. "You're not some random guy from New York. You're a respected doctor, you're Phog Allen's grandson for god sake, your name is on the building we are trying to get the rules in."

Mark continued to rebut my attempts over the phone. So I headed to the Charlotte airport for a flight back to Kansas so that I could get in front of him in person. I knew that I had to get Mark Allen to come to Austin if I had any shot at convincing Booth. And not just convincing him to bid, but convincing him that this was worth spending more than a million dollars on.

It wasn't until 11:30 p.m. that I pulled into the Allen driveway. A long layover had made getting from North Carolina to Kansas City an all-day event. Still, Mark and Louise fully understood the severity of our predicament and got out of bed to let me in.

Wasting no time, I played the video testimony from Larry Brown and Roy Williams for the Allen's. It was clear that they were both touched by the coaches strong opinions on the rules. I could sense that Mark was about to cave-in. When Louise finally said, "Mark . . . you have to go," he could no longer resist. He agreed to to come to Austin with us the following day.

Wednesday, December 8: Austin, 2 Days Until Auction

After landing in Austin, I drove Mark to the Dimensional Fund Headquarters. I had arranged with Deborah Foster for Mark to meet David at his office before the two men would head to the Booth home for dinner. Mark would be spending the night with the Booth's before continuing on to Florida for a medical conference the next morning.

I wanted to be there with Mark and David in the worst way, but I knew I couldn't. This was about the two of them meeting, two men whose surnames graced the greatest basketball venue in the world.

In the parking lot of David's office I considered how far Mark had come. When I had first spoken to him by phone in Las Vegas, he had been completely indifferent to the whole thing, annoyed that his wife had dragged him on the line. And now here he sat in the rental car outside of Dimensional's Headquarters, two cameras staring him square in his face.

"What do you think your grandfather would say about all of this?" I asked Mark.

"He'd be right here," said Mark. "So would dad."

"Dad" was of course Bob Allen, Phog's son who had been a standout basketball player for the Jayhawks in the early 1940s. By the time Mark got to KU, basketball players were too tall, too athletic, and too skilled for him to follow in his father and grandfather's footsteps. Instead, Mark focused his attention on following Phog and Bob in another way: as a physician. Though it had no bearing on his involvement, I considered that this was a chance for Mark to have a profound effect on the program he loved, like his father and grandfather before him.

As I watched Mark walk into the Dimensional offices, carrying the hopes of the Jayhawk Nation, the ball was now firmly in his hands. A century prior, James Naismith had put the ball in Phog Allen's hands. Naismith had invented basketball, but he knew he could only take the game so far. It was up to his young protégé to turn basketball into the worldwide phenomenon they were certain it could become.

Phog succeeded on behalf of his mentor by taking basketball to the world stage. Allen went on a fervent crusade and after a long fight eventually succeeded in getting basketball included as part of the 1936 Olympic Games. In a final gesture of friendship and respect, Allen started a fundraising initiative called Penny Day, where a percentage of proceeds from ticket sales to basketball games around the country was sent to Lawrence so that Naismith could attend the Olympic Games in Berlin. Phog's Penny Day campaign was a huge success and Naismith flew to Berlin where he threw up the first jump ball in Olympic history. Allen's testament to Naismith had served as a fitting final chapter and the perfect way to honor his legacy. Here we were, two generations later, with a chance for another Allen to honor James Naismith's legacy once again.

Thursday, December 9: 1 Day Until Auction

After a sleepless night, I waited desperately to hear from Mark. Every possible scenario ran through my mind, most of them bad. Why hasn't he called? Did he not want to tell me the bad news? Was there bad news? What had David said? What had David's wife Suzanne said? Why didn't I go? Should I have gone? Was I even invited? What was going on?!!

Daymion, Avi, and I headed down the highway to a local Austin diner to have breakfast. Once we were seated, my phone rang with a call from Mark Allen. Mark was finally alone. He told me that the evening had gone "pretty well." He said the Booths were lovely people and wonderful hosts. He felt lucky to have had the chance to go into their home and share the history of both his grandfather and Dr. Naismith, as well as make a case for how important it would be for the rules to end up at KU. But he finished with, "honestly Josh, I'm not sure where we stand. It seems 50/50 at the moment. If the school were more on board with this, so too would be David. Would you believe Bill Self didn't even call David back when he left a message for him?"

I was shocked to hear that. Bill Self had long been the missing link in all of this. We had heard from past coaches, players, etc. But for Self to not call back the school's most important alum seemed a bit strange.

"Mark, have we done everything we can?" I asked.

"I think we have," he responded.

Mark was now at the Booth house waiting to leave for the airport to continue onto his medical conference in Florida. I shared the news with Daymion and Avi and we sat there in silence. Five minutes later, my phone rang again. It was Mark Allen.

"Josh you're not going to believe what I'm about to tell you."

"What?" I replied, fearing bad news.

"I just hung up with Bill Self. I called him on his cell and was lucky enough to get him."

Mark proceeded to explain that as he sat in Booth's Austin backyard he couldn't help but wonder where Bill Self would be on all of this. Self was a guy who had a deep understanding and appreciation of the history at Kansas. But Mark wondered: Did he care about the rules? Like all Kansas fans, both the Allen and Booth families had enormous respect and admiration for Bill Self. If he wanted these rules, if Coach Bill Self thought they might help the program, then Mark had to find out.

Mark explained to Self that he was at David Booth's house and that there was an auction the following day. Self knew about the auction but had no clue what was going on. He was unaware that there was someone like myself bugging prominent coaches and alumni, had no idea that David Booth was interested in bidding on the rules, and didn't know that Mark Allen was caught in the middle.

"Gosh Doc, are you kidding me? To have the rules would be absolutely huge," Self told Mark.

"Well, why didn't you call David back?" asked Mark.

"David called me?"

"He left a message with your assistant earlier this week."

"He did? I didn't get the message. Let me see what's going on."

Self called Mark back immediately. It turns out in the midst of a very busy time for the basketball office, a simple miscommunication had kept Self from not getting the message from David. Self told Mark he would call Booth immediately to both apologize and share his endorsement.

"I think Coach is on board with this thing," said Mark. "Now . . . we've done everything we can."

Only a select few people can call the head basketball coach at the University of Kansas on his cell phone. And only an even smaller group of people would have that phone call answered by that same coach. Perhaps only Dr. Mark Allen would be addressed by that coach as "Doc," the same name that fellow coaches, administrators, and players used to address his legendary grandfather. I felt lucky that I had Doc on my side.

Half an hour later, Deborah Foster called. "David just hung up with Bill Self," she said. "We are on for tomorrow."

11

THE MIRACLE

WITH ROY WILLIAMS off to Carolina, the Kansas faithful turned to interim athletic director Drew Jennings for hope. While various names within the coaching ranks surfaced as possible candidates, one person seemed to separate himself from the pack: Bill Self.

Bill Self was the head coach at the University of Illinois where he'd been for three seasons, guiding the Fighting Illini to two Big Ten titles and three NCAA Tournament appearances. Self had been born and raised in Oklahoma and had played collegiately at Oklahoma State where he had been a solid player for four years.

After his playing career, Self joined Larry Brown's coaching staff at the University of Kansas, taking the position vacated by John Calipari. Self remained at Kansas for one season before returning to Oklahoma State where he served as an assistant for the following seven years.

As a head coach, Self had been a winner at Oral Roberts, Tulsa, and then Illinois. KU fans loved the fact that he was part of the "Kansas family," albeit for only one season. If Self came to Kansas he'd be leaving behind an Illini roster full of talent and a heralded incoming recruiting class. He'd also be faced with the difficult prospects of following in the footsteps of Roy Williams, a legend.

But for Self, Kansas was his dream job, and he decided that he was indeed up for the challenge. On April 21, 2003, William Jefferson Self was named just the eighth coach in the history of Kansas basketball. "I see this as a chance to sit in my opinion, and it's a biased opinion, the most prestigious chair in all of college basketball," Self said that day.

While KU lost two lottery picks in Kirk Hinrich and Nick Collison, Self inherited a squad of quality players like Aaron Miles, Wayne Simien, and Keith Langford—guys who'd played in two consecutive Final Fours. Self also welcomed a highly touted freshmen class whose commitments he succeeded in keeping, despite the coaching change.

Growing pains were evident in year one for the coaches, players, and fans alike. Self's style was a far cry from the frantic pace that Williams had deployed, which fans and players had grown to love. Under Self, KU's play appeared muddled at times and many of the players fought to resort to their successful past ways. Kansas finished tied for second in the Big 12 league race, behind Self's alma mater, Oklahoma State.

Despite the unsatisfying league race, the Jayhawks marched all the way to the Elite Eight to face Georgia Tech where they came an overtime away from advancing to their third consecutive Final Four. The loss, while disappointing, came on the heels of a postseason run that gave us hope that Bill Self was indeed the right man for the job.

The next two years made us question that optimism. Though Self led the Jayhawks to back-to-back conference titles in '05 and '06, the Jayhawks were unceremoniously eliminated in the first round of the NCAA Tournament. The first year Kansas fell to Bucknell while the following year the Jayhawks lost to Bradley University.

Meanwhile Roy Williams had finally broken through to do what we all expected he would eventually do. Roy had led North Carolina to its first National Championship since Dean Smith had done so in 1993. Watching Roy finally cut the nets down was like pouring salt on an open wound.

In 2007, Kansas won the conference again and faced UCLA in the Elite Eight. The Jayhawks finally seemed prime to take Bill Self to his first ever Final Four. In the media, Self's tournament history had begun to take on a life of its own. He had guided three programs to the Elite Eight: Tulsa, Illinois, and Kansas—but each time he'd failed to advance to the final weekend. Now in this his fourth time, surely things were to change. But they didn't. Kansas lost to UCLA and went home disappointed yet again.

In 2008, Self's fifth squad appeared to be his best team yet. Self's roster proved that he could recruit nationally with players like Mario Chalmers from Alaska, Darrell Arthur from Texas, Russell Robinson from New York, and Sherron Collins from Chicago. The Jayhawks marched to their fourth consecutive Big 12 title and entered the NCAA Tournament as a number one seed for the second year in a row.

When the 2008 tournament began, I had zero expectations. I was waiting for the inevitable collapse that had defined my March for twenty years. It had been exactly that long since Danny Manning had led Kansas to a miraculous National

Championship in '88. It had been twenty years of winning more games than anyone else in college basketball, only to come up short when it mattered most.

In the first round I expected the Jayhawks to be tested by a tough Portland State squad. But they weren't. In the second round I expected the Jayhawks to be challenged by a skilled UNLV squad. But they weren't. In the Sweet Sixteen I expected Kansas to be pushed to the brink by a talented Villanova team. But they weren't. As I headed to a KU-anointed bar in New York, I expected the Jayhawks to not only be tested in the Elite Eight. I expected them to lose.

This game had "loss" written all over it. We would be going up against the game's marquee Cinderella story in Davidson, a tiny school out of North Carolina led by tournament darling Steph Curry. Curry had led the #10-seeded Wildcats to the Elite Eight by dismantling various defenses including Gonzaga, Georgetown, and Wisconsin. Curry had done it inside and out, where his deep-shooting barrage set a record for most made 3-pointers in NCAA history. Davidson seemed like just the kind of team that had given KU trouble in years past: a well-coached mid-major, schooled in fundamentals that would not do anything to beat itself.

There was more. As the fourth and final Elite Eight game that weekend, all the other Final Four participants had punched their dancing tickets to San Antonio. All three of them had been number one seeds. Never before in the history of the NCAA Tournament had four number one seeds advanced to the Final Four. This history-making feat now fell squarely on the shoulders of the Kansas Jayhawks.

If that wasn't enough, there was even more pressure than the players wanting to make a Final Four for their coach, a winner at every level who'd somehow still never been there, or for KU rounding out the number one seed field in San Antonio. If the Jayhawks were to win, they'd face the North Carolina Tar Heels, coached by Roy Williams. Such a matchup would set the stage for a myriad of intriguing storylines, two basketball giants meeting on college basketball's biggest stage.

And if all of that wasn't enough, there was, believe it or not, even more. Oklahoma State had just fired their basketball coach Sean Sutton, the son of former coaching great Eddie Sutton. Media reports already confirmed whom the Cowboys would be keying in on to replace him; none other than one of their own, Bill Self. Knowing the Oklahoma State athletic department was flushed with cash and the backing of oil magnate T. Boone Pickens, it seemed to be inevitable that Self would return home, just as Roy Williams had done five years prior.

All of the above suggested that Kansas would come out against Davidson extremely uptight. And they did. Through the first ten minutes, the Jayhawks scored only 6 points. Steph Curry was predictably torturing Kansas on the way to 15 first half points. But the Jayhawks were able to hang tight with tough defense and a stellar first half from guard Mario Chalmers. At halftime, KU led by a basket at 30–28.

In the second half both teams wrestled to seize control as the lead changed hands on seemingly every possession. With twelve minutes to go the Jayhawks crawled out to a 6-point advantage on a Brandon Rush basket and free throw. But behind Steph Curry, Davidson fought back to grab a 4-point lead with just over seven minutes remaining.

KU bounced back to take a 6-point lead with one minute to go. Still, I waited for the predictable collapse to come. When

Davidson got fouled and cut it to 5, I expected it. When Steph Curry got wide open to swish a three to cut the lead to 2, I was not surprised in the least. When the Jayhawks failed to score, giving Davidson and Curry the ball back with sixteen seconds, I was certain they would win with a three. Curry would pull off what was his destiny. Everything was on their side. The entire world was watching, waiting eagerly for David(son) to slew Goliath. And Goliath was once again being delivered on a silver platter in the form of a make believe bird called the Jayhawk.

As time ticked away Curry danced around the perimeter dribbling, looking for a gap to get his shot off. Here it comes, I thought. Three number one seeds were waiting in San Antonio for a fourth. Joining them was sure to be the #10-seeded Davidson Wildcats and their star guard Steph Curry. The clock ticked away. Eight seconds, 7, 6, 5 . . . it was clear that Davidson had no intention of tying the game. They were going for the three and the win. Kansas switched defenders on Curry, who was forced to pass to his teammate Jason Richards at the top of the key. The clock ticked down to three seconds. Richards had no choice but to let the shot go. The ball hung in the air. I knew it was going in. I just knew it.

I grabbed my jacket and got ready to leave. Not just the sports bar . . . but Kansas basketball. I couldn't take it anymore. Twenty years of torture, of my blood pressure suffering, of years being taken off my life, of depression and frustration and misery. I told myself that I was done once and for all. And so too would be Bill Self, homeward bound to Stillwater where he would inevitably lead the Cowboys to a National Championship.

Trying to convince myself I was ready to leave the Jayhawks forever, I moved towards the door. Richard's shot looked to be spot on target as the game-winner. In a moment's time it would swish through the net and a nation of basketball fans in love with Cinderella would rejoice

But it didn't. It fell left. It missed. Somehow, Kansas had won the game. Somehow, the Jayhawks had avoided another huge upset. We were going to the first ever Final Four to feature all of the number one seeds. The most stacked Final Four in history would include powers UCLA, Memphis, and the overall number one seed, North Carolina Tar Heels, a team that looked unbeatable.

Despite the win, I gave the Jayhawks very little chance in the next game against UNC. We all did. KU, while talented, had not one player selected for first-team conference accolades, let alone All-American ones. The media had continually harped on the Jayhawks lack of a "go-to guy," as their primary downfall. Carolina on the other hand, featured a deep, talented team, led by the collegiate player of the year, and consensus All-American Tyler Hansbrough. Despite our bearish outlook, my brother and I made plans to meet in San Antonio. We decided that if the Jayhawks had any chance at all, they needed us in the stands.

As if KU needed more distractions in addition to the media's obsession over a program finally facing the coach who had spurred them five years prior, news surrounding the Oklahoma State coaching vacancy had reached a new decibel level. Reports on ESPN had T. Boone Pickens and the Cowboys already prepared to offer an outlandish compensation package for Self to return home to his alma mater.

Still, there was no way around the simple fact that this would be one of the biggest games in program history. Roy had already won a title at UNC. Now he was on his way to another. Ironically, the team he guided for fifteen years stood in his way. Kansas fans had never wanted to win a basketball game more. But Carolina had barely been tested all tournament long, while KU had just barely escaped with their lives to get to San Antonio. Beating the Tar Heels seemed like the tallest of tasks.

Before Micah and I settled into our dome seats high in the heavens, we stood close to the court watching the real life drama unfold. We saw Bill Self walk out, here in his first Final Four, in the biggest game of his coaching career, against a man whose shadow he could burst out of, or fall behind. In terms of college basketball, this was reality TV at its finest: two coaches, two fan bases, and so much intertwined history.

What unfolded over the first half would have been utterly impossible to predict. Over a twelve-minute stretch, Kansas proceeded to play some of the most beautiful basketball ever played in an NCAA Tournament game, especially one with such high stakes. Coming into the game, many were concerned that KU would struggle to keep up with the pace of Carolina. Instead, the exact opposite ensued. Carolina looked stuck in the mud. The Jayhawks meanwhile were everywhere. It felt as if KU had two extra players on the court at all times.

Kansas decimated the Tar Heels in every facet of the game. Carolina couldn't score on KU's swarming defense. On the other end, KU couldn't miss, getting wide-open looks with ease. After leading by a modest 5 points at 15–10, the Jayhawks went on a 25–2 run to pull out to a 40–12 lead. 40–12! With five minutes to go in the first half, Kansas guard Brandon Rush was tied with the entire North Carolina team at 12 points a piece. During the television broadcast of the game, analyst Billy Packer exclaimed, "It's over." With more than half the game remaining Packer had called it for KU.

While UNC put forth a valiant fight, the hole proved to be too big to climb out of and the Jayhawks marched to an 84–66 victory. On the River Walk that evening, Jayhawk fans celebrated late into the night. It felt great to beat Roy. But so much would be riding on Monday's game against Memphis for the National Championship. As good as it felt to beat Carolina, second place meant little in the grand scheme of things. We simply had to win one more game.

The game against Memphis pitted Bill Self against John Calipari. Both had begun their coaching careers at Kansas. Both were protégés of Larry Brown. Calipari had emerged as the game's greatest recruiter, a salesman perfectly in tune with the Internet age of college basketball. With a slew of star recruits, he had turned the Memphis program into a perennial power and now he too was on the cusp of his first National Championship.

This would be a highly contested battle as both teams played a stingy brand of defense. We watched anxiously in the stands as Kansas grabbed a 33–28 lead going into the half. Watching from behind the Kansas bench was Roy Williams, with a Jayhawk sticker attached to his sweater. I wondered how Williams would feel if Kansas finally won it without him?

But that didn't look to be much of an issue as Memphis took complete control of the game down the stretch. Leading by 9 points with just over two minutes remaining, it looked all but over for the Jayhawks. All signs pointed to yet another loss in the National Championship game for KU.

A Darrell Arthur jump shot cut the lead to 7. KU then stole the in bounds pass and Sherron Collins hit a three to cut the lead to 4 with 1:45 remaining. Suddenly the Jayhawks had life.

Memphis responded, making two free throws to push the lead to 6 with a minute and a half to go. On the next possession two Mario Chalmers free throws cut the lead back to 4. With one minute to go KU's Darrell Arthur hit a turnaround jumper to cut the lead to just 2 points. But KU couldn't quite capitalize on their next possession and with just 10.8 seconds to go, Memphis star Derrick Rose walked to the free throw line to try and ice the game for the Tigers.

As Derrick Rose took the ball from the referee, I readied for the exit from my seat high up in the Alamodome, unable to bear the prospects of losing another title game. I considered what was at stake for the Kansas basketball program and its legion of fans. If Rose made both free throws our national title hopes would be lost once and for all. And with those hopes would likely go our coach, Bill Self, leaving behind a jinxed Kansas program for the greener grass of his old home in Stillwater. With a slew of seniors set to graduate and three more underclassmen likely to declare for the NBA, our roster would be wiped out. Standing near the exit, I suddenly had an epiphany of the worst kind: *We will never win it all,* I thought.

Even when Rose only made one of two free throws, I highly doubted KU's ability to score as Sherron Collins dribbled up court. When Collins handed the ball off to Mario Chalmers, as he fell to the ground in a near-botched pass attempt, I highly doubted Chalmers would hold on. With a hand directly in his face, falling to the left, deep behind the 3-point line, I highly doubted Mario's shot would come close to even touching the rim.

As the ball hung in the air for an eternity, I was certain the game was over. How could someone falling to their left, with a hand in their face, from so far out, make this shot? They couldn't. It seemed geometrically, scientifically, impossible. To make such a shot would seemingly go against the laws of gravity . . . of space and time and reality.

But then, as if steered by the hand of god, the basketball dropped perfectly through the net without so much as even gently caressing the iron rim. Somehow, some way, Mario Chalmers had tied the game with just 2.1 seconds remaining. Memphis threw the ball in bounds and from halfcourt took a shot for the win as time expired. It missed. The game was going into overtime.

Now, we miraculously found ourselves heading into overtime against Memphis in the 2008 National Championship game in San Antonio. The Jayhawks had used a manic comeback to overcome the 9-point deficit they faced with just over two minutes remaining in regulation. I stood near the exit high in the Alamodome, unable to calm my nerves and sit. The security guard standing nearby had all but given up yelling at me to return to my seat. It was clear to her that I would be standing the rest of the way.

My confidence was growing by the second. Memphis had let the title slip through their fingers. Kansas now had all of the momentum. Thirty seconds into overtime a Sherron Collins steal led to a Brandon Rush layup, giving KU its first lead since early in the second half. Darrell Arthur and Darnell Jackson then scored on subsequent possessions and KU's lead ballooned to 6. The Jayhawks never trailed again and ultimately sealed the victory at the free throw line. Micah, Daymion, and I rejoiced in the stands, in disbelief as to what we had just witnessed.

The anniversary had been lost on none of us. Twenty years to the day after Danny and the Miracles had won an impossible championship, Mario and his Miracle had done the same. It seems for great things to happen for the Jayhawk basketball program, some form of divine intervention is required.

The Journey

Friday, December 10: Auction Day

As I rose from my hotel bed to get dressed, I wondered if I had done everything humanly possible to put us in a position to win this auction. With all that had happened the past month, it seemed that whatever outcome would present itself on this day was no longer up to me. It wasn't up to Mark Allen, or the school, or even Bill Self for that matter. It was up to David Booth . . . and perhaps his wife, Suzanne.

"What about Suzanne Booth?" I thought. She was somewhat of an unknown in all of this. Mark had told me that she was genuinely interested in the rules and the auction. I knew getting her on board was critical. I sensed that she was someone who could sway David, like most wives. As we drove down the highway to Dimensional, I thought of the other alumni I had pitched and how they said they had to first run it by their wives. I thought of the other key women in this journey: my mom, who urged my dad to go ahead and spend the money on season tickets years before; Louise Allen, who'd dragged her busy husband into all of this against his will at first. Finally, I thought of my boss, Maura, who had given me over two weeks away from work to try and accomplish a dream.

As we pulled into Dimensional Fund Advisors, I thought of Dr. James Naismith. His boss, Dr. Luther Gulick, had also given him two weeks . . . two weeks to come up with the impossible, a new game to be played indoors. . . .

For the first part of the two-week assignment, Naismith tried to interest the class in every existing game, all of which failed. Naismith next tried to modify outdoor games like football and soccer to see if they could be played indoors, but they were far too rough to be played on the hard gymnasium floor.

On the next to last day of his two-week assignment, Naismith met the class with no idea of what they were going to do for their sixty-minute period. He gave the students no instructions, leaving them completely on their own. When the period ended, Naismith watched solemnly as they filed out of the gym and into the locker room. "With them," he thought, "went the end of all my ambitions and hopes."

With weary footsteps, I mounted the flight of narrow stairs that led to my office directly over the locker room. I slumped down in my chair, my head in my hands and my elbows on the desk. I was a thoroughly disheartened and discouraged young instructor. Below me, I could hear the boys in the locker room having a good time; they were giving expression to the very spirit that I had tried so hard to evoke.

As Naismith listened to the locker room chatter through the narrow floor, he tried to retrace his attempts of the previous two weeks to develop a game that would interest the class. He realized his attempts to modify existing games had failed because the students and other athletes enjoyed those games as they were and did not want to mess with tradition.

Continuing to sit at his desk, even after the students had left the locker room and moved onto their next class, Naismith next thought about games "from the philosophical side." Pondering games as a whole—rather than individually—he started to draw some conclusions.

All team games that he could think of involved a ball. So, whatever new game was to be invented should have a ball of some kind. But he knew there couldn't be tackling because doing so indoors would lead to injury. Then something suddenly occurred to Naismith: If running with the ball were disallowed, then tackling wouldn't be necessary. For his new game to work, the player holding the ball would have to be stationary.

With a few ideas starting to make sense, there remained much more to figure out, namely scoring and the type of goal to be used. Naismith considered the goals used in lacrosse, but such a stationary goal would undoubtedly cause injury with players whizzing balls by one another's heads to score. Football's field goals and end zone goal lines appeared to present a watered-down brand of rugby football. Naismith recalled his days at McGill University, leading two teams of offseason rugby players in the competitive throwing of a ball into an empty box laid upon the floor at the end of the gym. But the defensive strategy in these games circumvented all offense, with defenders crowding around or even sitting in the goal to prevent any scoring from taking place.

Then Naismith recalled a game from his youth called "Duck on a Rock." All the boys would line up ready to throw a rock in an attempt to knock it off another rock, with "the duck" sitting atop a boulder. If their toss successfully knocked off the duck, they had to retrieve their stone and return to base before the guard could pick up the duck and tag the thrower. If the boy's throw was unsuccessful, the thrower had to retrieve his rock before the guard tagged him.

If the boys fiercely threw their rocks in a straight line and missed the duck, the rock would often land too far away for them to retrieve it and return to base safely, before the guard could tag them. The most effective strategy was for throwers to arch their toss, so that if their rock missed, it wouldn't land too far from the boulder, allowing them to quickly retrieve it. Touch, accuracy, and finesse became much more important to success than sheer force.

And then a light bulb went off inside Naismith's head. He would use an elevated receptacle as a goal and would position it above the players' heads. With the ball thrown in an arch, offensive players could surmount defensive efforts with a touch of deft accuracy. The goal would be small, so that the touch of the thrower would prove paramount over brute force, which in turn would minimize the game's roughness as Naismith had intended.

Though he had almost reached the end of the two-week time constraint, Naismith immediately felt confident in what he had. He felt his game had met all of Dr. Gulick's requirements. It was compelling enough to keep the young men interested. It was safe enough to play indoors. And it was simple enough that anyone could play.

With the class set to meet the following morning, Naismith imagined the game in his mind. He began to formulate a series of rules.

1. There would be no running with the ball.
2. No tackling or rough body contact would be allowed.
3. Players would be free to secure the ball and throw it in the goal at any time.

Naismith showed up to school early the next morning with two crucial elements to still figure out: What type of ball would be used and what would the ball be thrown into? Upon entering his office, he noticed a football and soccer ball lying on the floor. He grabbed the soccer ball for its roundness, deciding it would be the perfect ball for his new game. He hurried down to the gym to address the goal situation when on his way he ran into the school janitor, Mr. Stebbins. Naismith asked him if he had two wooden boxes he could use for a new game, knowing if anyone had such receptacles, it'd be Stebbins, known for his container hoarding. Stebbins thought for a moment and replied that he had two wooden peach baskets in the storeroom that might work well.

Stebbins brought the peach baskets and, upon Naismith's initial inspection, they seemed perfect. They were small like Naismith had wanted, fifteen inches in diameter. Naismith marched them to the gym, hammer and nails in hand. He went to the balcony that overhung the gymnasium floor, reached over the ledge, and secured a basket at each end of the gymnasium, roughly ten feet above the floor below. Pleased with the peach baskets securely fastened high above the hardwood, Naismith hurried back to his office to scribble down the rules for his new, still untitled game.

Minutes before his class was to meet, Naismith sat down to his desk, pencil in hand, and began to scribble down a set of simple yet fundamental rules. He handed the notes to Ms. Lyons, the departmental secretary, so she could type them in time for the approaching gym class. In this frantic last minute exercise, Naismith came up with thirteen rules, all of which seemed to cover every last facet of the game he could anticipate. Ms. Lyons quickly began typing the first rule. As the key hit the paper, rule number one read: "The ball may be thrown in any direction with one or both hands . . ."

Just before class began, Ms. Lyons handed Naismith the second typed page and he hustled down to the gymnasium. As he tacked both pages to the bulletin board just as the class was filing in, James Naismith was unsure of what he had.

On December 10, 2010, nearly 119 years after the rules were pinned on the gymnasium wall of the YMCA in Springfield, I walked into Dimensional Fund Advisors, unsure of what I had. I first greeted David Booth's assistant, Deborah Foster, who had been something of a guardian angel sent from above, helping me along the way. I also greeted Suzanne Booth, David's wife. Finally, I was introduced to David's friend, Bill Bradley, the former senator from New Jersey and a Hall of Fame basketball player who had led the New York Knicks to two NBA Championships in 1970 and 1973. In some perfect version of the universe aligning, Bradley happened to be visiting David on this day, a visit that was totally unrelated to the auction about to take place.

As we dialed Sotheby's from the speakerphone in David Booth's private conference room, my heart pounded like never before. I wanted to sit down next to David or Bill Bradley or Suzanne, but I couldn't. Instead, I stood against the back wall as our dedicated Sotheby's phone attendant began to relay the scene unfolding before her.

Two auctions had just concluded. The first was for Robert F. Kennedy's copy of the Emancipation Proclamation, signed by Abraham Lincoln. Selling for nearly $3.8 million the sale price would set a new record for any presidential document ever sold at auction. The second item was General Custer's Last Flag: The Culbertson Guidon, from the Battle of the Little Bighorn. This American treasure had sold for just over $2.2 million. On this historic day at Sotheby's, the realized sale price of the first two items had exceeded both auction estimates.

Last but not least were the original rules of basketball. Considering the high amounts just fetched for two iconic pieces of history, I hoped that the exact opposite would transpire for the rules. For Sotheby's, I hoped the rules would be a colossal failure, a monumental disappointment. I prayed that on this day, no one other than David Booth had any interest in acquiring James Naismith's original rules of basketball.

Ian had mentioned he had put a reserve on the auction, an amount for which he would not sell the rules for less than. If the winning bid was not at or above Ian's reserve price, then he would have the right to maintain ownership of the rules. I had no clue what Ian's reserve was, but the figure that continually looped in my head was one million. One million dollars was the amount that Booth had pledged when we first had met a week prior. Considering Bill Self was now aware and fully backed his efforts, I figured Booth might perhaps go a bit higher. But how much, I was unsure.

I assumed the bidding would start in the low hundreds of thousands. From there I expected it to increase in increments of $50,000 at most. This assumption had no legitimate base in reality, as I had never attended an auction, listened to an auction, or even watched one on television.

The sound of applause came through the speakerphone from the live crowd gathered in New York. "They've brought a Harlem Globetrotter out," explained our phone attendant.

From Austin, I couldn't see legendary Globetrotter Curly Neal rotate on the auction stage much to the crowd's delight. Even if I could have witnessed Curly famously spinning a basketball on his finger, its amusement would have been lost on me. Now that the moment was here, I could hardly breathe, let alone chuckle at the sight of a Globetrotter.

It had been a little over one month since I had learned of this auction, and now I stood in a conference room connected to the office of KU's most powerful alumnus, David Booth. I considered what it would look like if I had a heart attack on the spot.

The intensity in our phone attendant's voice did little to calm my nerves. Her tone was polite, but businesslike. She put forth an impression of someone who had been here before, but at the same time knew the seriousness of what was about to transpire.

"You're there, right?" she asked, the auction imminent.

"Yes," replied David Booth.

"The rules will begin now," she said.

How would Booth play this? I wondered. *Would he survey the activity or would he jump right in?*

Deborah had mentioned that David and Suzanne had previously bought art at auction, but I wondered if they were up to this particular challenge. I knew Booth had launched an investment company famous the world over, but could he handle the pressure of an auction for the most important sports document in the history of mankind?

I was readying myself for that first amount to come through. *Would it open at $200,000? Perhaps it would it be as high as $300,000. It couldn't be more than $300,000 . . . could it?*

Then, before I knew it, a number came through the speaker-phone as clear as day. I would have sworn I was hearing things, had the look on Daymion's face not confirmed my disbelief. "1.3," our phone attendant had said.

1.3?! 1.3?!

I wanted to fall to the floor. I wanted to pull my hair out. I wanted to cry. But there was not time for me to process "1.3." There was no time for me to try and understand how my hopes and dreams were all but crushed. There was no time, because our phone rep immediately continued to relay the bidding activity. "1.4," she said. "1.5."

1.5?! 1.5?!

Hope seeped out of me and I felt the harsh reality settle in. We were out of it before it began. I had been fooling myself all along. Running around like a crazed-lunatic, like a chicken with my head cut off . . . and for what? Nothing.

I felt bad for wasting David Booth's time. Clearly he would kick us all out and move on with his day. I just wanted to immediately leave. No awkward, drawn out, long goodbyes. I just wanted to go.

But standing behind Booth, something suddenly occurred to me. He wasn't standing up. He wasn't turning around to tell me "sorry." In fact, Booth hadn't moved at all. He had remained seated. Unflinching. "When I want to bid, how would you like me to handle it?" he calmly asked our phone attendant.

"I'm telling you what's going on and you tell me when you want to come in," she said. "We're at 1.5, now 1.6, 1.7, would you like to say 1.8?"

"Yes I would," responded Booth.

And just like that, my emotions did a complete 180. I no longer felt weak, in fact I felt the opposite. I felt like Rocky Balboa finally getting in a punch on Ivan Drago after suffering through a relentless beating. *Not so fast* I wanted to scream. *Let's do this!* I wanted to say to Booth as if he was my brother and we were in the stands at Allen Fieldhouse, but I couldn't. David Booth wasn't my brother, and this wasn't Allen Fieldhouse. This was a respectable place of business. I had to use every ounce of restraint to hold it in.

"1.9," the attendant immediately replied. With this counter bid, I turned pale. I felt the air canal in my throat closing. I had returned to a state of desperation.

"Would you say 2?" our rep asked Booth.

"Yes," he replied.

Yes we will! I thought to myself. *Goddamn right we'll say 2.* I wanted to give Booth a high five. I wanted to urge him on and get him fired up. But still, I couldn't. All I could was just stand there and remain completely and utterly . . . helpless.

I waited for 2.1 to come in. The bidding had accelerated at lightning speed, and I assumed the next counter would follow suit . . . but it didn't. There was a pause. The first since the auction had started. "There is someone that was bidding . . ." our attendant said, as if a main competitor had now dropped out. *We could be on the verge of a win*—until the words "2.1 on the phone," interrupted my premature celebration.

Ughhh! I can't take this anymore! My heart was beating out of my chest. I could hardly breathe. This bipolar swing of emotion was simply too much for me to handle. I feared Booth was getting close to his limit. I figured Suzanne couldn't possibly keep supporting this. She hadn't gone to KU. She wasn't a basketball junkie. At some point, rational thinking was sure to win out. But when David was then asked, "Would you say 2.2," he responded quickly and confidently with, "yes."

"2.3 on the phone," our attendant immediately relayed. "Would you say 2.4?"

"Yes," fired back Booth.

"2.5. Would you say 2.6?"

"Yes," replied Booth again, without so much as looking up from the speakerphone.

Despite the ballooning price, I was starting to feel better about our chances. It seemed that I had underestimated Booth's commitment. I knew how important this was to me, but I was starting to realize just how important this was to him as well.

"2.7," the attendant reported. "Would you say 2.8?"

"Yes," replied Booth.

"You're competing against one other phone now," our attendant relayed. This struck me as good news. Though I knew nothing of the other party's financial situation, the fact that it appeared to now be down to us and one other bidder seemed positive.

I wondered, was it the Smithsonian? A document collector? Perhaps it was an NBA team owner? What was this other party's motivation?

I knew about my motivation. I knew about Booth's motivation: the most tradition-rich basketball program in history. A program started by the game's inventor, Dr. James Naismith.

I thought of Dr. Naismith. I couldn't help but think of him as he was looking right at me. For good luck, I was holding a picture of Naismith standing atop the KU campus aiming a ball at a peach basket. It was an iconic photo shot during the late years of his life. It was a photo I'd seen hundreds of times. But this one had special meaning as his grandson Ian had given it to me when my journey began.

"They went to 2.9," our attendant then said.

My stomach dropped. Doubt returned. It seemed that whomever we were bidding against wanted this just as bad as us. I looked at the picture in my hands and began to pray for help.

"Would you say 3?" our attendant asked Booth.

To this question, there was finally a pause from David Booth, the first one of the day. I could certainly understand his hesitation. Here we were, a million dollars over the auction estimate and two million over his initial pledge.

Standing behind Booth, I couldn't see his face. I couldn't read his emotions. Not only did I feel helpless . . . I felt lost. I was trying to read Daymion's face, Avi's eyes, Suzanne's body language. I glanced in Bill Bradley's direction. I couldn't sense anything. Or maybe I could? It seemed bad. Was it bad? It didn't feel good.

"Yes," Booth finally replied, with a hint of uneasiness in his usually confident voice.

I could hardly bear the scene playing out before me. How did I end up behind Booth? I couldn't have picked a worse place to stand in the entire room. One thing was for certain, I could no longer stand there and attempt to read Bill Bradley, Suzanne Booth, or peek in the direction of Daymion and Avi, who were faced with the impossible task of trying to film while this was all unfolding. I decided to cover my face with the picture of Naismith . . . and pray some more.

I listened for an update from the speakerphone, as did everyone else in the room. *What is taking so long?* I had always just assumed auctions were meant to progress at a rapid fire pace. But it seemed that for this auction, Sotheby's was actually waiting for the competition to respond.

Finally, our Sotheby's rep chimed in. "They went to 3.1. Would you say 3.2?"

"Yes," responded Booth, returning to his unwavering ways.

The waiting game resumed. It seemed whomever we were up against was having second thoughts about continuing. Seconds passed. Each one felt like a minute long. Why Sotheby's was simply waiting for their response seemed inconceivable to me—and to Booth as well. "What are they doing, figuring out the square root of something?" he finally asked no one in particular.

"Come on hammer it," our phone attendant said.

Hammer it! I thought to myself. *Hammer it!*

"They went to 3.3," said our phone attendant.

Ughh!!! How could she get my hopes up like that!?

"Would you say 3.4," she asked.

"Yes . . . but tell them to speed it up if you wouldn't mind. This is getting a little bit . . . off," Booth replied.

Like myself, Booth seemed to be using his best efforts to practice restraint, but he was clearly growing more frustrated with the time Sotheby's was allowing the other side.

"I think they said no," relayed our phone attendant, again doing her best to get my hopes up prematurely.

"I wouldn't count on it," replied Booth. "There'll be at least one more."

He was right.

"They went to 3.5," she confirmed. "Do you want to say 3.6?"

This lady is literally killing me, I thought. *Why is she adding her own commentary? KEEP IT TO YOURSELF!*

"Let me think about it," said Booth. "I don't know if I want to do it or not."

This was the moment I had feared all along. Though it had arrived far later than I expected, it had still arrived. While Booth's commitment, his fight, his determination had far exceeded my wildest expectations, with what was at stake, there would be no moral victories. Coming in second place would be of no comfort to me or the Jayhawk Nation. Like a National Championship game, this was an all or nothing scenario.

"What do you think, Suzanne?" Booth finally asked his wife. Though I couldn't see her give the thumbs up from behind the picture, Booth's response let me know she had remained supportive.

"Okay, 3.6," said Booth.

It was back to waiting. "You want to drop out or bid?" said Booth, his gentlemanly disposition being tested. "I don't know what's so complicated."

"They went to 3.7," finally said our Sotheby's rep.

Booth was no longer frustrated, he was downright mad. "Can you ask from your phone on the floor, why it is that he (the auctioneer) is taking so much time?"

"I can't out loud," she responded. "But I can give you an equal amount of time," she said.

I could sense Booth's utter disdain for this auction, a disdain that turned quickly into a palpable silence. Booth thought alone for a moment.

"Okay where is it?" Booth finally asked.

"It's at 3.7," she replied. "And I can say if you'd like to bid 3.8?"

"Okay 3.8," said Booth somewhat reluctantly.

It felt like we were getting close to Booth's limit. That, or he was so turned off by Sotheby's handling of the bidding that he no longer wished to continue. Either way, it seemed we had reached a tipping point of some sort.

The waiting game resumed yet again. While we couldn't hear the auctioneer through the phone, it was clear that he was milking the two bidders for every last penny.

"Okay it seems as now they'll hammer it," said our attendant. I put no stock in this latest prediction from our personal Nostradamus, and waited for the counter to come in.

Except it didn't.

The auction had begun with three devastating syllables, "One. Point. Three." But it ended with three glorious ones. "They. Are. Yours," said our phone attendant when the gavel finally went down. I didn't know what to do. I put my hands in the air and went to hug David Booth.

I could not begin to comprehend what had just happened. It didn't seem real, none of it: the journey, the auction, the victory, the champagne that followed. But it was. Standing behind David and Suzanne Booth and their close friend, Bill Bradley, we had indeed phoned in the winning bid for the original rules of basketball. The buyer's premium brought the total sale price to a whopping $4.38 million, setting a new world record for the highest-priced piece of sports memorabilia ever sold.

It turns out I had had very little grasp of David Booth's emotional connection to his roots: the house he grew up in on Naismith Drive, his family, his parents, and the University of Kansas. "What they don't know is I would have paid twice as much," Booth told me after the auction had ended. I hugged him again for pulling off a miracle. I looked down at the crumbled picture of James Naismith in my hands and I knew he was with us in the room.

I eventually floated out of Dimensional Fund Advisors enjoying a high I hadn't felt since the last time I was in Texas. That high had come in 2008 when KU had pulled off an incredible comeback to beat Memphis en route to the National Championship. By the time we made it to the San Antonio Riverwalk to meet up with other Jayhawk fans, it had sunk in. "We are National Champions!" I remember saying to Daymion and Micah as we poured champagne all over ourselves.

But this still had not hit me. There was no gathering of Kansas faithful waiting for us on 6th Street in Austin. Shortly after we arrived at a bar to celebrate, we were shocked to see my wife holding my daughter as she was interviewed for the Nightly News just following the auction (she had attended in New York and the media had caught wind of the story). As I looked up at her on TV alongside Katie Couric, it still didn't feel real. When we finally made it back to our hotel room late that evening, it still had not hit me what had happened.

The next morning, as I lay in my hotel room bed half-awake, it felt like it was all just one big dream I had imagined. Then the phone rang, waking me up for good. On the line was John Engstrom, the owner of Scheimpflug Digital in New York. On the strength of his friendship with Daymion, John had donated the services of his employee, Avi, as well as a bevy of film equipment to the project. News of our triumph had reached him and he was dying to get through and congratulate us.

Thanking John, I suddenly felt a wave of emotion come on. John's selfless act had proven to be an absolutely integral part of the whole equation. In fact, it was selflessness from many that had made this all possible: Daymion, my wife, my colleagues, Maura. After barely keeping it together with John, the phone rang again. This time it was Maura. She and her crew had been covering the New York side of the auction the day before.

If John put me on the verge, speaking to Maura sealed the deal. Shortly after our conversation began, I completely broke down into tears. Like John, Maura had never once set foot in Allen Fieldhouse. She had no emotional connection to KU, James Naismith, or Kansas basketball. But she had a connection to me. She had a connection to the right thing happening. And so she supported my crazy quest from the start. Her support made me never have to make a tough decision to quit my job to pursue this. She did something one in a thousand people would have done—she let me go.

About the same time I was having an emotional meltdown, David Booth received an email of particular note. This email was from a friend of David's whom he sat on the board with at the University of Chicago School of Business. Like Booth, this man had received his graduate degree from Chicago. The email from this man was quick and to the point. "I may have cost you some money," it said.

The email was from David Rubenstein, who had been on the other phone line, bidding against Booth the day before. Rubenstein, the CEO and co-founder of The Carlyle Group, one of the largest private equity firms in the world, had made headlines for his past purchases of iconic American documents. He had bought a copy of The Emancipation Proclamation and put it on display in the Oval Office. He had bought a rare copy of the Declaration of Independence that he put on display at the State Department. In 2007, Rubenstein made headlines when he had purchased the last privately owned copy of the Magna Carta at a Sotheby's auction for $21.3 million. Rubenstein's Magna Carta now resides at the National Archives in Washington, D.C.

As for the rules, Rubenstein was reminded of the auction by the president of his alma mater, Dick Broadhead. Hoping the rules would make it there after he won, Rubenstein was bidding on behalf of that same alma mater. In 1970, David Rubenstein graduated magna cum laude from Duke University.

Basket Ball

12

THERE'S NO PLACE LIKE HOME

THE NEWS OF David and Suzanne Booth winning the original rules of basketball immediately spread like wildfire. News outlets everywhere ran with the story. Soon after the auction had ended, KU released a statement from Chancellor Bernadette Gray-Little, which read:

> *We are delighted to learn that David and Suzanne Booth have acquired Naismith's Rules of Basketball, a piece of sports history that is intertwined with the University of Kansas and its storied tradition of basketball excellence. Naismith was KU's first coach and started what would become one of the winningest college basketball programs in the nation and certainly the most tradition-rich.*

With their beloved coach Bill Self behind it, the University was finally—once and for all—on board with the rules coming home. Now the only questions that remained were when the rules would get there and how would they be displayed?

But David Booth made it known almost the minute the gavel went down that he, for one, was in no hurry. Booth told school officials that he would not simply hand the rules over. Instead, he challenged the university to build the proper venue to house the historic document—a structure that would finally bring to life Naismith's tremendous legacy at the university and beyond. One thing was certain; KU needed leadership within the athletic department to meet Booth's challenge head-on.

A few weeks later, Kansas finally found that leadership when they hired an athletic director to fill the position that had been vacated over five months before. In Sheahon Zenger, they found just what they were looking for: one of their own. When Zenger, born and raised in nearby Hays, Kansas, spoke at his introductory press conference, he said, "It's good to be home."

Zenger was also thrilled to step into the rules initiative:

I look at this as a gift. For this to be laid on my desk on day one is an opportunity and a blessing . . . and I can't wait to get started. My earliest memories are several blocks just to the south of Allen Fieldhouse. For these rules to come home it has a special significance for me and I couldn't be more honored or more excited to be a part of this project. Now, we can create something here that is truly unmatched in the world of college basketball.

With costs for the addition to house the rules estimated in the $18 million range, Zenger appears to be just the man for the job. It seems that it finally took a Kansas boy to grasp the enormous significance of having the original rules of basketball on the KU campus.

Soon after winning the auction, I was finally able to meet with Kansas coach Bill Self. Our meeting was to take place in the Naismith Room, upstairs in a newly remodeled wing of Allen Fieldhouse. As I pulled into the parking lot of the legendary gymnasium, I thought back to 2008 when Self led the Jayhawks to an incredible national title. After the ensuing pandemonium, Self finally sat down with his alma mater, Oklahoma State, and listened to what they had to offer.

Ultimately, Self decided to stay in Lawrence. He said after making his decision to stay that "home had called, but Lawrence, Kansas is home now." So that's where I picked up with Coach Self.

"What does home mean for you?"

"Well, home is where the roots are dug in," he said. "Home is a place where, it's not just a stopover until you get your next place. Home is where you fully intend to stay. And so that's why I think it's so important for us to have the rules because the roots are dug deep here and they're not coming out."

"What will having the rules mean for the basketball program?"

"Well, when we add this, it becomes the focal point of our university. This is not an athletic department deal. This is a university deal. It's a recruiting tool for basketball and our athletic department and it's a recruiting tool for our entire university and will generate a sense of pride for every alum, for everyone that's ever taken a class here, everyone that's ever given a dollar here, and everyone that's ever supported or bought season tickets. They can beat their chest a little bit. This is something that nobody else has and nobody else will ever have.

"What do you make of David Booth's challenge now to the university, to build a proper addition to house the rules?"

"I agree 100 percent with David and I agree 100 percent on him purchasing the rules, but I agree with him 100 percent that we have to do our job to deserve to house the rules. We have a new athletic director, Sheahon Zenger, who's hungry. He's not going to back down from anything and I think things in our athletic department have been shaky, rocky, for the last eighteen months because of some things that have gone on. Those times are behind us. It's time to move forward. It's time to move forward in a big way and this is the big first step."

By this point, Coach Self understood most of what had transpired with my mission to bring the rules home. So I was curious what he thought. "What did you think of my journey, my mission to get the rules?"

"I think you're nuts," he said. "I think you're nuts," he said again. "But the thing about it is, nobody gets anything done unless they're a little nutty, unless they have great energy and great enthusiasm. So from my standpoint, I love coaching players like you. I love coaching guys with personality. I don't want duds. I want guys that add something, bring some excitement to the table and I will say firsthand, you have certainly done that."

To hear Coach Self say that was the ultimate icing on the cake. (Even though he was probably playing to his audience.) After wrapping up with Self, I left the Naismith Room, jumped into my rental car, and headed down Naismith Drive. I drove past Naismith Hall, the building I had lived in while attending Kansas Basketball Camp during the summers of my youth. I drove just down the road to 1931 Naismith Drive and stopped in front of the tiny house where David Booth had spent the summers of his youth. I thought about what a remarkable story

David Booth was, how incredible it was that a man could emerge from such humble beginnings and one day through hard work and determination, be in a position to purchase a legendary, iconic artifact for the university he loved.

It occurred to me how much Naismith and Booth shared in common: two visionaries who had conquered the world, yet at their core neither lost the down home goodness instilled in them at a young age. It occurred to me how this quality was precisely what made my home state of Kansas and its inhabitants so special.

Before leaving town, I had one more stop to make. I continued down Naismith Drive, took a left on 23rd Street and another left on Massachusetts Street. I had driven down Massachusetts Street, the main drag through downtown Lawrence, hundreds of times over the course of my life. But until this moment, I had never considered how appropriate the name was. "Massachusetts." The game's birthplace sat at the heart, served as the main artery of a town defined by the sport of basketball.

I turned down 15th Street and pulled into the Memorial Park Cemetery. I parked and made my way to the very back of the graveyard. There I found James Naismith, resting next to his wife, Maude. Naismith's gravestone, like Booth's home, was simple and humble, and in no way, shape, or form an indicator of the miraculous life he lived. It's just how he would have wanted it.

As I sat in front of Naismith's grave, I thought back to Roy Williams who used to jog by the graves of Naismith and Phog Allen on game days. "I wanted some divine help from God. I was doing it to try to help us win games," he had told me.

I had also asked Coach Williams about his own place of burial. "Had you stayed at Kansas the rest of your career, do you think you would have been buried in Lawrence one day?"

"Well, if I had stayed there . . . yeah, probably so," he replied.

I had asked Roy that uncomfortable question because of something said to me by Dana Anderson, the first alum I had pitched on my journey. Anderson lived and worked in California, a state he had resided in for decades. But he had a striking response when I asked him about his home.

"Kansas is home," he said. "It will always be home. We consider ourselves temporary residents of California. We will be buried in Lawrence, Kansas."

The more I thought about Dana's statement, the more I realized how much it cut to the heart of the matter. I had asked everyone I had met about home, but maybe it was Dana who got it right. Maybe home is not where you currently reside or even where you're born and raised. Perhaps home is where you want to be buried.

Roy Williams will be buried in North Carolina. So too will his mentor, Dean Smith. I for one hope Bill Self will one day be buried in Lawrence, Kansas, just like Allen and Naismith.

I thought about where I would eventually be buried when my time on this earth was up. My family's plot had been located in Kansas City, just adjacent to the temple where I had my bar mitzvah. Then I remembered Las Vegas. While in Vegas, I had my undying commitment to Kansas basketball forever emblazoned on my arm in the form of a tattoo. More than aware of the old rule that stipulates those with tattoos not being suitable for burial in Jewish cemeteries, in that impulsive moment I was forced to make a decision. In the end, I chose Jayhawk over Judaism. Some 120 years prior, James Naismith had done something similar. He'd chosen a career in athletics over one in the ministry, a decision he likely never regretted.

And I don't regret my tattoo. I don't care if they won't bury me in a Jewish cemetery. I know where my home is. When I die, you can spread my ashes across the hallowed ground adjacent to my temple, Allen Fieldhouse, a house of hoops that served as the gathering place for the most profound religious experiences of my youth, the place I still dream of every day from my temporary home in New York.

EPILOGUE

A **FEW MONTHS AFTER** winning the rules, the Jayhawks entered the 2011 NCAA Tournament as one of the prohibitive favorites to cut the nets down. The year before, KU had also been a heavy favorite as the overall number one seed. That year, the Jayhawks had lost in shocking fashion to upstart Northern Iowa in the second round.

But this year was sure to be different. KU had comfortably moved through the first three rounds without being closely challenged. Now, the Jayhawks had to simply slide past the outmatched, mid-major Virginia Commonwealth in the Elite Eight to reach the Final Four.

On Sunday, March 27, Daymion arrived at my New York City apartment to watch the game. I didn't know it at the time, but he had already bought our plane tickets for Houston, the site of the 2011 Final Four. He was going to surprise me after the game, certain it would make for another glorious, life-altering adventure deep in the heart of Texas.

We were optimistic that the winning of the rules would change KU's unfortunate history of high-seed disappointment. After all, we had the holy grail of hoops in our possession (or on the way rather), and we were hopeful that this good omen would put to rest our tournament demons. But it didn't. The Jayhawks were shockingly upset by VCU, and for the second year in a row, lost to a lower seed.

A stunned Daymion called the airline to try and cancel his reservation. I felt stupid for getting my hopes up, for already looking into Final Four tickets and hotels and Houston bars that Jayhawk fans frequented. I should have known better. We all should have. After all, there is simply no way around the fact that to be a Kansas fan means you will often suffer come March.

There is no way around the fact that, for a school with the most winning seasons, the most Hall of Famers, the most first-team All-Americans, the most conference championships, and the longest current streak of consecutive NCAA Tournament appearances, this too is a program that has been plagued by postseason underachievement. This is a program that lost in the 1953 NCAA title game by one point to Indiana. This is a program that lost in the 1957 NCAA title game by one point in triple overtime, and those Jayhawks had a pretty decent player named Wilt Chamberlain on their team.

So many more years of misfortune came to mind. There were #1 seeds in '86, '92, '95, '97, '98, and '02, just to name a few. In 2003, Kansas lost to Syracuse by 3 points in the title game after missing 18 free throws. Without hesitation, Kansas should have at least double the amount of national titles than it currently has.

Losing to VCU bothered me for the same reason that losing to Northern Iowa had the year before. It had been another golden opportunity to add to our championship pedigree, a pedigree that often doesn't get the respect it deserves because of our low title ledger.

But something unexpected happened: I quickly bounced back after the loss to VCU. Whereas such a loss would typically send me into a deep, lengthy depression, this time it didn't. Shortly after Daymion left my apartment, it occurred to me, once and for all, that the high stakes, winner-take-all nature of the NCAA Tournament is just one measuring stick. Alongside this narrative of postseason disappointment is a narrative that can never be taken away from us Jayhawks. A narrative that in the pantheon of sport, is truly one-of-a-kind as a program started by the game's inventor, Dr. James Naismith. After the devastating loss, I found solace in the rules, knowing that their impending arrival at KU would be paramount for the university's basketball legacy.

To me, the only other place the rules would have made sense was the Naismith Memorial Basketball Hall of Fame in Springfield, Massachusetts. Rumors said a certain Hall of Fame benefactor did indeed bid on the rules, but dropped out before the price reached two million dollars.

I had never been to the Basketball Hall of Fame prior to the auction, and had only heard stories about its supposed unstable financial footing and lackluster surroundings in the down-trodden city of Springfield. So after the KU season ended, I decided to mosey on up to the Hall and check it out firsthand.

Upon entering Springfield, I decided to first go to the corner of State and Sherman Street. It was at this intersection where the

YMCA Training College once sat, where in 1891, an American invention occurred which would soon take over the world. As I approached the site, I saw another American invention that has since taken over the world. On the corner of State and Sherman, on the exact location where James Naismith introduced basketball at the YMCA, there now sat a McDonalds.

After leaving the "Big Mac of Basketball," I journeyed through the city of Springfield towards the Hall of Fame. On my way, I noticed what many people had mentioned to me before: that Springfield was a town that had certainly seen better days. As I approached the Hall, it seemed very nice from the outside: a modern structure complete with an enormous basketball-shaped annex. This latest version of the Hall came to be in 2002, and is connected to a strip mall of sorts housing restaurants and shops.

After checking out some of the exhibits, I sat down with John Doleva, the president of the Hall of Fame, and asked him what he thought about the rules:

> *Well, there is definitely a side that feels this was where the rules belong. We have items that are on loan and we get things that are just outright donated and you have to accept that. We don't go out and we don't purchase, whether we could afford to or not because once you start buying memorabilia as a museum then no one donates anymore and we really want people to feel the tug of I'm giving back to the game. We have a replica set of rules here, we explain the story, and I think most visitors are very satisfied with that. They get a sense for just exactly how close those rules are to today's rules and what a creative set of rules they were from James Naismith.*

Though Doleva wouldn't concede that Kansas made as much sense as Springfield, he did have this to say: "I think Kansas and Springfield share a great bond. The game was invented here, but perhaps it grew up in the Kansas area and then sprouted from there."

After touring the rest of the exhibits, I sat down with Matt Zeysing, the Hall of Fame's resident curator and historian. Zeysing graduated from, of all places, the University of Kansas, which struck me as incredibly appropriate. (Of course the historian at the Basketball Hall of Fame attended the foremost basketball finishing school in the country.) I was especially eager to hear from Zeysing, a man seemingly caught between two great basketball institutions.

> *I think it's appropriate that the original rules of basketball have found a home at the University of Kansas, because the Naismith legacy will last forever there. To have them on display there is not just meaningful for the university, and for the people of Kansas, but for any basketball fan that comes through there.*

Zeysing thought for a moment before adding one final thought. "There's a starting point there. I've often said that the game was invented in Springfield, Massachusetts, but perfected in Lawrence, Kansas."

While Zeysing wouldn't say whether one place was more appropriate than the other, he did have this to say: "Allen Fieldhouse is the greatest place on earth. If you go to a game on Saturday, means you don't have to go to church on Sunday."

Though he didn't know it, Zeysing's adage hit right at the heart of my argument. Twenty times per year, when the Jayhawks play at home, James Naismith comes to life in one of sport's most electric environments. Each and every game, 16,300 screaming fans channel Dr. Naismith from their hearts to the top of the rafters. He is in every cheer, every scream, and every "Rock Chalk Jayhawk" that is chanted. While the Basketball Hall of Fame is an incredibly interesting place, filled with some great pieces of basketball history, it does not match that feeling inside Allen Fieldhouse on game day.

It has been well documented that Naismith wanted the Basketball Hall of Fame to be built in Lawrence. With the rules there, he will finally get his wish.

I have since been fortunate enough to speak to some other Kansas legends about the rules coming back to KU. "The day that the rules go on display, it's going to be a great day in Kansas basketball," said my all-time favorite Jayhawk, Danny Manning. "We have a nice museum now, I think it will be enhanced 100 times when people are able to walk in and see the rules, walk into Allen Fieldhouse and see one of the best college gyms in the country."

Manning chimed in on how special it was for a guy who grew up on Naismith Drive to pull this off for his alma mater. "Just knowing that Mr. Booth was someone that would come around the Fieldhouse and watch the games, and be part of the university, for him to go out and have all the success he's had and share that with all of us by getting the rules is unbelievable."

Legendary Jayhawk radio broadcaster, Max Falkenstein, who called games from 1946 to 2006, agreed with Manning.

What an accomplishment for David to do that for the university and for all the people of Kansas and for the nation of America. It's a treasure that's really indescribable in terms of what it's going to mean to the people of Kansas and to KU in particular. It's perfect to recognize Dr. Naismith in Allen Fieldhouse because of his association with KU basketball. I mean, no other place in the world could match James Naismith Court in Allen Fieldhouse. You can talk about Indiana and Duke and UCLA and North Carolina but nobody can even come close to matching the history and the tradition of KU basketball.

I knew a couple of KU guys would agree with me, but I wondered what an impartial journalist would think? So I sat down with Alexander Wolff, a senior writer from *Sports Illustrated* with a unique vantage point on the rules. Wolff's 2002 *SI* article "The Olden Rules" had long been considered the seminal expose on the game's founding document.

Wolff put a touching spin on the outcome of the auction:

If I'm James Naismith and I'm peering down at what happened to these two typescript pages, that after an all-nighter get fatefully get tacked up on that bulletin board, and I'm watching this kid (David Booth) growing up on Naismith Drive who's sneaking into Allen Fieldhouse to watch basketball games and then by dent of industry, hard work, makes enough money to bid on these rules and deliver them back to KU, well, then, I think I'd be pretty pleased.

Wolff's words struck me as incredibly powerful. But most telling and most important to me are not what the legends or the players or coaches or the scribes have to say. For me, the most satisfying part of this has been hearing from regular Jayhawk fans like myself. Thousands have reached out to me via every form of communication imaginable to express their deepest gratitude, how proud they are to be Jayhawks, and how much having the rules in Allen Fieldhouse will mean to them and future generations.

Which brings me back to the man who saved the day, David Booth. I hadn't fully grasped David's love for KU until I witnessed him on the day of the auction. But still, post auction, after the heat of the moment had subsided, I wondered if he harbored any regrets about the whole thing?

"I never realized how much satisfaction this would bring me," he said. It's a game changer; it's one of these forks in the road in life where life is a lot better if you take it. The excitement that we've gotten from this, you just can't put it into words. When something like that happens it enables you to reconnect with so many of your friends from school. I've heard from a lot of people I hadn't heard from in years so it's been terrific.

It makes me particularly happy that this has brought so much satisfaction to David Booth and his family. I feel incredibly fortunate to know the Booths, the Allens, and to have made so many new friends on this amazing adventure. Being able to meet a slew of legendary Jayhawk players, coaches, and personalities has been beyond my wildest dreams. But for me, personally, I think the most fulfillment will come years from now, when I take my grandkids to Allen Fieldhouse and show them Dr. James Naismith's original rules of basketball and think back on the dream Jayhawk journey I went on. Maybe by then it will have sunk in.

Rock Chalk Jayhawk

AFTERWORD

TEN YEARS AGO, I was faced with a tough decision: come to the University of Kansas, or stay as head coach at the University of Illinois. The truth of the matter is we had a great thing going at Illinois and were on the verge of having an unbelievable team. But at the end of the day, I thought about this: Ten years from now, would I wake up and say, *I could've been the head coach at Kansas—the place where it all started from a collegiate standpoint.*

It's now ten years later, and I wake up and think how right that decision was and how incredible it's been here. If the history of the game means anything to you, there is no better place in all of basketball than Allen Fieldhouse on Naismith Drive. With the original rules on their way, it's about to get even better.

I feel a special connection to Dr. Naismith because he started the basketball program at Kansas, becoming our first head coach. Along with Dr. Forrest "Phog" Allen, Naismith promoted the game at KU and spent the rest of his life in Lawrence, where he is buried just down the street from the university. It's pretty incredible that I'm just the eighth coach in 115 years of basketball at the University of Kansas.

The one thing that makes our program so special is our incredibly passionate fan base. If you're a KU fan, Jayhawk basketball is a way of life. You wake up with it. You go to bed with it. It is a part of you every day. Of course, alums from many different schools feel a similar connection . . . but it's unique here. It's unique because of an unparalleled history and tradition. A tradition started by the game's inventor, Dr. James Naismith; a tradition that Kansas fans take a tremendous amount of pride in. So how appropriate is it that a group of Jayhawk fans took it into their own hands to secure Naismith's original rules for the tradition they love?

That brings me to Josh Swade. I told Josh that I think he is nuts . . . because he is. But it's a good kind of nuts, as this was a situation that needed someone like him to take the lead on. He went on a journey that took a tremendous amount of grit and determination. I'm not so sure I've heard of a fan doing something similar for the program they love. And make no mistake about it, Josh loves Kansas basketball.

The stars aligned when Josh made contact with Phog Allen's grandson, Dr. Mark Allen. The day before the auction, Mark gave me a call and informed me of all that was going on. After Mark and I spoke, I immediately called David Booth to voice my support.

When I spoke to David, I tried to tell him what having the rules would mean to each and every alum that has ever given a dollar to this school; what it would mean to every student that's ever attended a class here; and certainly what it could mean to us as a basketball program. David said, "I don't know how much it'll go for." But then he said something to me that I'll never forget. He said, "but you know what? I'm pretty competitive. And I'm not used to losing."

I knew right then and there that we were going to win. I knew we'd win because I knew that David would get in there and fight; and I knew he would not give in because he loves his alma mater. This school has changed him, so why can't he do something to help change it? For a guy who grew up on Naismith Drive and came from very modest means, I can't imagine a more storybook ending than this.

David, his brother Mark, and their families have been very generous over the years; first with the building of the Booth Family Hall of Athletics—which is as first class a facility as you will find in college athletics—and now with the rules. Having the rules here at Kansas will bring Dr. Naismith's legacy full circle. It will allow us to properly honor him, Dr. Allen, and tell the story of Kansas' unique role at the epicenter of the game of basketball.

But make no mistake about it . . . this is bigger than athletics. This will have a positive impact on our entire university, our entire community, and our entire state for generations to come. This will elicit a deep sense of pride in every alumnus, every season ticket holder, and every individual that calls Kansas home. We have an opportunity to create one of the greatest tourist attractions in this area of the country and when the DeBruce Center is complete and the rules are here, you'll be able to stop all the arguments.

Allen Fieldhouse will take its rightful place as the undisputed mecca of college basketball.

Bill Self
Head Basketball Coach
University of Kansas

ACKNOWLEDGMENTS

I'D LIKE TO thank the following people for their love and support: Lauren, Stella, Lucy, Gertie, Mom, Dad, Grammy, Shanna, Jonathan, Micah, Samantha, Brad, Janis, Paul, Amy, and the extended Swade, Schwartz, and Moffatt families.

All of my friends, new and old. Maura Mandt for her belief in me. Dave Chamberlin, Jen Aiello, Gina Paradiso, Anthony Behn, and everyone at Maggie Vision for all of their enthusiasm and hard work. Matt O'Connor for seeing it through. My brothers on the road, Daymion and Avi.

Mark, Lou, Chris, James, Chad, and the entire Allen family.

David, Suzanne, Mark, and the entire Booth family.

John Engstrom, Deborah Foster, Mike LaChapelle, Justin Unell, Amy Hawley, Todd Leabo, Kevin Kietzman, Jesse Newell, Drew Gooden, Steve Nash, Alvin Gentry, Alexander Wolff, Seth Davis, Blair Kerkhoff, Danny Manning, Max Falkenstein, John Hadl, Jay Bilas, Dick Vitale, Dana Anderson, Stewart Horesji, Cole Aldrich, Selby Kiffer, Leila Dunbar, Michael Zogry, Rabbi

Arthur Nemitoff, Bill Bradley, Bill Self, Larry Brown, Roy Williams, Matt Zeysing, and John Doleva.

My appreciation goes out to Kari Stuart and Jason Katzman for making this book a reality. I'd like to thank John Walsh, John Skipper, Connor Schell, Erin Leyden, Wright Thompson, and everyone at ESPN.

Everyone at Spencer Research Library, Rock Chalk Video, Springfield College Archives, and the Naismith Hall of Fame: Sheahon Zenger, Nicole Corcoran, Hoanie Stephens, Chris Theisen, and everyone at the University of Kansas.

I'd also like to thank the late Ian Naismith and the entire Naismith Family. I'd like to thank Amos Alonzo Stagg for making a recommendation that would set in motion the greatest basketball tradition of all time.

I'd like to thank James Naismith for taking that job and starting the program.

I'd like to thank Phog Allen for building it up.

I'd like to thank all the coaches and players who have put their heart and soul into it ever since.

And lastly, I'd like to thank Jayhawk fans everywhere. This is for you.

This book is in memory of Louis, Anceley, and Scott Swade.

SOURCES

The following works were incredibly useful in writing this book:

Books

Kerkhoff, Blair, *Phog Allen: The Father of Basketball Coaching*. New York: Masters Press, 1996

Naismith, James, *Basketball: Its Origin and Development*. New York: Association Press, 1941

Rains, Rob with Hellen Carpenter, *James Naismith: The Man who Invented Basketball*. Philadelphia: Temple University Press, 2009

Rice, Russell, *Adolph Rupp: Kentucky's Basketball Baron*. Urbana: Sagamore Publishing, 1994

Self, Bill with John Rohde, *Bill Self: At Home in the Phog*. Olathe: Ascend Media, 2008

Smith, Dean, *A Coach's Life*. New York: Random House, 1999

Stark, Doug, *The SPHAS: The Life and Times of Basketball's Greatest Jewish Team*. Philadelphia: Temple University Press, 2011

Webb, Bernice Larson, *The Basketball Man: James Naismith*. Lawrence: University Press of Kansas, 1973

Williams, Roy, *Hard Work: A Life On and Off the Court*. Chapel Hill: Algonquin Books, 2009

Articles

Wolff, Alexander, "The Olden Rules," *Sports Illustrated*, Nov. 25, 2002

Websites

kuathletics.com: University of Kansas Men's Basketball Media Guide

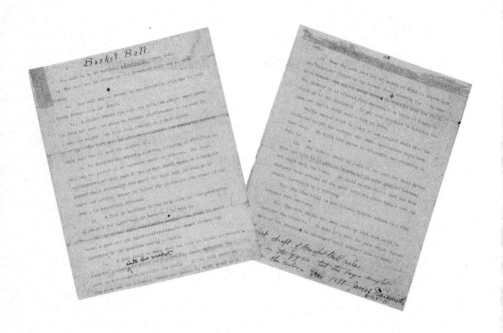